Praise for Christina

Fully understanding our relationship to technology is a vital question for all of us as humans. Christina is ready to have that conversation.
–Tiffany Shlain, Emmy-nominated filmmaker & author of *24/6: The Power of Unplugging One Day a Week*

In a culture barraged by the trends of hustle, tech, and self-improvement crazes, Christina Crook not only reminds us what it's like to be human—but gives us a much-needed road map to feeling like a whole one.
–Jess Davis, founder of Folk Rebellion

JOMO isn't a trend—it's the future for our families, friendships, and communities. The coming decade is going to be all about learning the tools Crook shares here. This book is inspiring for anyone who wants to remember—or learn— what it feels like to be a whole person.
Read it and share it.
–Sarah Selecky, Giller Prize-nominated author of *Radiant Shimmering Light & This Cake is for the Party*

Once again Christina Crook shows us that the one thing we shouldn't miss out on is her heartfelt, soulful thoughts on where we can tap into the joy around us.
–David Sax, author of *The Revenge of Analog: Real Things and Why They Matter*

GOOD BURDENS

HOW TO LIVE JOYFULLY IN THE DIGITAL AGE

CHRISTINA CROOK

NIMBUS PUBLISHING LTD.

— NIMBUS.CA —

For Michael

Nimbus Publishing Limited
3660 Strawberry Hill Street, Halifax, NS, B3K 5A9
(902) 455-4286 nimbus.ca

Edited by Whitney Moran
Designed by Heather Bryan
Cover illustration © Sandra Javera
Printed and bound in Canada
NB1580

An earlier version of the chapter Be Amazed first appeared as "The School of Wonder: Why we need to keep feeding our curiosity" by Christina Crook, for *UPPERCASE* magazine.

An earlier version of the chapter Be Brave first appeared as "Learning trust in the sharing economy" in *Religious News Service*.

An earlier version of the section "Ten People, One Shower: We met on Twitter and our families moved in together" first appeared on CBC.ca.

Library and Archives Canada Cataloguing in Publication

Title: Good burdens : how to live joyfully in the digital age / Christina Crook.
Names: Crook, Christina, author.
Identifiers: Canadiana (print) 20210230363 | Canadiana (ebook) 20210230797 | ISBN 9781771089784 (softcover) | ISBN 9781771089852 (EPUB)
Subjects: LCSH: Goal (Psychology) | LCSH: Intentionalism. | LCSH: Motivation (Psychology) | LCSH: Joy. | LCSH: Technology—Psychological aspects.
Classification: LCC BF505.G6 C76 2021 | DDC 153.8—dc23

Canada

Nimbus Publishing acknowledges the financial support for its publishing activities from the Government of Canada, the Canada Council for the Arts, and from the Province of Nova Scotia. We are pleased to work in partnership with the Province of Nova Scotia to develop and promote our creative industries for the benefit of all Nova Scotians.

A Word of Welcome

This book is for you, the...

- city dweller burned out on keeping up with the Joneses
- executive burned out on toxic hustle
- creative exhausted by placing shadow work in front of eyeballs in exchange for likes
- marketing director who can't sleep for all they're shilling on the internet each day
- parent, educator, or caregiver who has witnessed the diminishing effect of tech on kids
- person seeking a path to meaning and joy in an overwhelmed world

My dearest hope is that this book teaches you to love, to know that caring for your small corner of the world matters, and helps you channel your energies online and off toward *good burdens*: caring relationships, community, and creative projects that bring joy.

Welcome, friend.

Introduction

Laziness is the opposite of love. Love is effortful.
—Scott Peck, *The Road Less Travelled*

My need for quiet rises in the folds of mid-morning. My hands stack papers sorted then filed. The handwork is a kind of mind-work, decluttering the mess of the early day. Of running up and down stairs seeking mittens and children. Of tending to hot pans and smears of toothpaste. Of walking home in crisp air, tripping over the long-tired lists already running through my head.

I sit on the floor and sort.

I start many workdays this way. Tell myself that if the room is tidy, my mind will tidy; my thoughts will lie out flat, my heart rate slow, my soul quiet.

But the truth is, it doesn't work.

For all the outer order, my inner landscape remains desolate. Shame lurks in corners, assuring me my work is of little worth. I sit at a tidied desk swarmed with fear.

No, the quiet space is farther. It's buried beneath my ribcage, a sharp point in my fleshy centre. I have to get down on the floor, on all fours. Knees bent on hardwood desperate for mopping, elbows jutting down while hands lace up in prayer. My head comes low, all the way down to the floorboards, and I must call out.

I call out for the Great Quiet. I call out to the Star of the Sea. She is the settler of storms. He is the calm for these waters.

I need quiet, yes. A silence within. An empty ark on a Monday, needing to be filled.

Our days are full.

For most of us, from the moment we wake up in the morning our days are ripe with noise, busyness, and rushing. At the end of the day, we are tired. So very exhausted.

Can you relate to any of these feelings?

- I'm tired of trying to keep it all together. My team needs me. My spouse needs me. My kids need me. I feel like I am already living with a wall of regret.

- I'm exhausted. I'm on 24/7. I feel like I can't turn off because if I do, my career will slow down and my boss will think I'm lazy and I will miss my dentist appointment and I'll never get my side hustle off the ground.

- I come home from work feeling numb. The only thing I have energy for is scrolling and Netflix. And more Netflix. And more Instagram. And more Facebook. At the same time. I've been on social media long enough to know it's a waste of time but I. CAN. NOT. STOP. I don't know what else to do.

We want a simple lifestyle, but we also want all the comforts of the rich. We want the depth afforded by solitude, but we do not want to miss anything. We want deeper connection with loved ones, but we also want to watch television and grow our social media following.

"Small wonder," writes Ronald Rolheiser in his book *The Holy Longing*, "life is so often a trying enterprise and we are often tired and pathologically overextended. Medieval philosophy had a dictum that said: Every choice is a thousand renunciations. To choose one thing is to turn one's back on many others."

It takes a powerful no to say a powerful yes.

Happiness is Love, Full Stop

In 1938, Harvard University started following 268 male under-graduate students in the longest-running study of human development in history. The goal of the Harvard Study of Adult Development, often called "the Grant Study," was to determine what factors contribute most strongly to human flourishing. Harvard researchers measured their subjects on everything: personality type, IQ, drinking habits, family relationships, even "hanging length of his scrotum." *Everything*.

The head of the study, psychiatrist and professor Dr. George Eman Vaillant, published the findings from the study, which is ongoing, in his 2012 book, *Triumphs of Experience*.

The factor of life success Vaillant refers to most often is the powerful correlation between the warmth of a subject's relationships and their health and happiness in later years. What the study specifically found was that men who were most satisfied with their relationships at age fifty were the healthiest at age eighty. Research participants who scored highest on measurements of "warm relationships" earned an average of $141,000 a year more during their peak salaries than those who scored lowest. They were also three times more likely to have professional success worthy of inclusion in a Who's Who list. Of the findings, *The Harvard Gazette* wrote: "Good genes are nice, but joy is better."[1]

If there's any part of you rolling your eyes right now, you're not alone. In 2009, Vaillant's insistence on the importance of this variable was challenged, and he returned to the data for re-analysis. Not only did he find that he had accurately correlated the quality of relationships to well-being, he determined that it was even more closely linked than he had previously thought.

Vaillant measured warm relationships as *having close friends*, *maintaining contact with family*, and *being active in social organizations*. In relating this to the Grant data he said, "it was the capacity for intimate relationships that predicted flourishing in all aspects of these men's lives."[2]

After seventy-five years and $20 million spent on the Grant Study, Vaillant concluded that the key to human flourishing can be summed up in five simple words:

"Happiness is love. Full stop."

The Change

I see happiness on the face of one young man in my neighbourhood.

His name is Sam, and he lives down the street and around the corner from me and my family. For at least an hour each morning and every afternoon, he stands out on the sidewalk. I learned Sam's name after nearly a year of us smiling at one another, saying hello and chatting briefly about the weather, politics, or whatever was on Sam's mind that particular day. I asked him his name so I could write it down on the little neighbour map I keep at home so I would remember.

I don't know Sam well, but I do know he is a young adult and is around the house most of the day. His speech is a little slow and sometimes he has a hard time fully forming his thoughts. But Sam's always got opinions. About the neighbourhood. About the weather. About government (and the giant political sign hammered in his family's front yard). And he's always sharing them with the biggest, brightest smile in the world.

I think a lot about Sam. He's my favourite fixture of our neighbourhood. I look forward to travelling down his block on foot, by bike, or even in my car, just so I can see his face. He always has a smile for me. Always.

What is Sam out there looking for?

Before the COVID-19 pandemic, I saw a way of life so at odds with the human experience I often found it difficult to breathe. I saw us belittling our human vulnerabilities, addicted to distraction, trying to life hack (doesn't it just *sound* terrible) away our imperfections to keep pace with our machines. I saw us out for ourselves. Worst of all, I saw Silicon Valley billionaires abandoning the world—*us*—altogether by building bunkers in New Zealand and shooting past the moon to reboot civilization.

I saw a world with no time for a person like Sam.

COVID-19 helped us change.

As if startled from slumber, we awoke to the truth that it's all so very fragile, these limbs, lives, life.

The change helped us recall some things.[3] We remembered:

- That we don't need to spend much money at all.
- That we are deeply tied to and dependent on the natural world.
- That humanity could be better if we wanted to be.
- That being kind is the only thing that matters.
- That we can easily make most of the food we buy.
- That we are good at distancing from our emotions.
- That we keep chasing things we really don't need and are way too indifferent to what happens to each other. We are even strangers to ourselves!
- That we are doing too much we didn't enjoy for the sake of doing.
- That our needs are far fewer than we think.
- That hours in a day can increase if we just slow down.
- That we rely on the outside world to tell us how to behave, think, and feel.
- That our families need us more than we thought they did.
- That we can actually save the Earth, if we want to, without spending a single penny, just by staying home.
- That almost everything we do is non-essential.
- That adversity and fear bring out the best and the worst in people. Both lurk in the deepest part of each of us, and we must decide which will prevail.
- That relationships are important. Life sucks if you do it alone.

We've changed.

I see signs of the change all around my neighbourhood. Literal handwritten signs. There's the makeshift *Where's Waldo* search-and-find propped on a nearby lawn to entertain neighbours out on a distanced walk by. There are *The Ministry of Silly Walks* directives instructing pedestrians to *STOP* and proceed only with their goofiest footwork. There are the *Black Lives Matter* and *Thank you, Essential Workers* missives plastered across living room windows. There's the wild-looking tiger cutout propped in the tall grass of our own yard with a speech bubble intended for our gentle-hearted mail carrier that says, *Thank you. We can do this.*

I've watched neighbours spill out of houses onto front porches and set up camp—the new outpost, the respite from the tyranny of video calls, wild indoor thoughts, and rage-inducing news.

We've come outside to see if the world, if *we*, are really still here.

We're still here.

The Trade-off

Sometimes you need someone else to ask the question to discover what's really true about you.

Not long ago, Nigerian-born Canadian Ony Anukem invited me on her *Twenty5 Podcast* to ask me what I wish I had known when I was twenty-five. Ony is smart. I intentionally arrived at our recording time unprepared, hoping to let my answers slip out naturally instead of spouting canned responses the way I sometimes think I should. (*Got to stay on message. Got to hit the talking points.*) As I shared my circuitous career path through public broadcasting, freelancing, communications, publishing, and early parenthood, I heard myself tell her this:

> All of the best things that have happened in my career and in my life had nothing to do with me controlling them.

A wave of shock reverberated through my body as I heard myself say these words. In an instant, I saw how my efforts to *control* had so persistently let me down and how everything meaningful and good in my life had come by some other means entirely. They all had something to do with openness, a wild trust in my instincts, and, I'd go so far as to say, serendipity: meeting the right people at the right moments.

I want more good in my life, more meaning and joy. Don't you? If I couldn't control my way to those outcomes, what *could* I do?

Technology reinforces our impulse to control.

On an average day, you and I spend more time with our digital products and platforms than we do with any single human being. Because of this, we constantly put ourselves in the way of the three sirens of consumerism: *comfort, control, and convenience*—the drivers of Big Tech, Big Corporations, Big *Everything*. Over time, they've shaped the way we think about relationships, the way we work, create, and even the ways we're willing to love.

But what is the cost of this constant orientation toward comfort, convenience, and control? Over time, these systems constrain what we are willing to do.

You know that the act of creating, of making anything worthwhile—whether it be a family, a resilient mind, a vocation, a marriage, a vibrant neighbourhood—doesn't work like that. There's nothing efficient or comfortable about it.

All of the best things that have happened in my career and my life had nothing to do with me controlling them. Chances are the same is true for you.

Here is what I'm getting at, Joy Seeker. The tech that shapes our lives is at odds with the way humans *actually work*.

At our core, you and I are after one thing: love. But here's the thing: love is the opposite of control. Laziness is the opposite of love. The way we experience love is through the inconvenient joys of relationship. Warm relationships are our greatest source of happiness and *relationships aren't easy, they're effortful.*

Comfort, control, and convenience, the promises of our tech-obsessed world, aren't going to get you where you want to go.

Think about it: the things you are most proud of in life—the child you are raising, the marathon you completed, the community garden you're starting, the major project you hit out of the park—these required all of you: all of your attention, all of your love, all of your courage, all of the risk. Could you control it? No. Were you all in? Hell, yes you were.

> The way we experience love is through the inconvenient joys of relationship.

It is in these great effortful pursuits that we experience not only the outer reaches of our abilities but our limits, requiring us to rely on others and in turn deepening our love of the people and projects that mean the most to us. They're *good burdens*.

The burdensome part of these activities is actually just the task of getting across a threshold of effort. As soon as you have crossed the threshold, the burden disappears.

And what are you left with then?

You are left with joy.

It's what you were made for.

Good Burdens

"What happens when technology moves beyond lifting genuine burdens and starts freeing us from burdens that we should not want to be rid of?" asks philosopher Albert Borgmann in his 1984 book, *Technology and the Character of Contemporary Life*. "If we believe that we, as humans, were created for relationship and meaningful work, work that provides for families and serves neighbors, work that engages our bodies and creative faculties, then it follows that we would value a certain kind of burden," he explains.

He called them *good burdens*, commitments that tether us to people and the physical world. Like the burden of preparing a meal and getting everyone to show up at the table, or the burden of reading poetry to someone you love or going for a family walk after dinner, or the burden of letter-writing—gathering our thoughts, setting them down in a way that will be remembered and cherished and perhaps passed on to our grandchildren.

Albert points out that these types of activities have been obliterated by the readily available entertainment offered by every screen in the twenty-first-century world.

Stepping out of your algorithm is essential to moving out of a set position and into relationship. Mary Clark Moschella, Roger J Squire Professor of Pastoral Care and Counseling at the Yale Divinity School, once told me: "The joy of being in relationship is that we step outside of ourselves."

It is that act of stepping outside of ourselves that often gets us unstuck; how do we move outside of a space we've inhabited for so long?

Reclaiming Effortful Living as the Path to Joy

This book is a reclamation of effortful living as your path to well-being.

In these pages, I'll challenge you to channel your energies online and off toward good burdens: caring relationships, community, and creative projects that bring you joy. Using historical

> The purpose of life is not to run away and avoid, it is to face life as you're living it and learn to love. What have you been avoiding?

data, real-life stories from leading mindful tech leaders, and a rich personal narrative, I'll make the case for increasing the intentionality in your day-to-day life, while offering concrete solutions for flourishing in the digital age.

As you'll see, the book is divided into five parts. The first section, The Algebra of Joy, examines the impacts of digital media and technology and what their efficiency-at-all-costs motives have really cost us. It explores the massive global shifts in the way we interact with one another and reveals how our addiction to tech is not a self-control problem but an environmental problem. So, in the first section, we step back to put our lives in context and unlock the two elements of joy.

Discovering what you love is one of life's greatest joys, and though you might not have known it, you've been doing it all your life. The second section, Discovering Your Joys, focuses on a necessary step on any journey: deepening self-awareness. Here you'll begin unlocking what makes you *you* and develop a positive relationship with your abilities and your limits.

Section three considers solutions for living in a wired world. It reveals how key shifts in your thinking can enable you to draw closer to yourself and others. You'll take an inventory of your close relationships, social groups, and daily scripts, asking: *are these life-giving or life-taking?* You begin Being Led by Joy.

Realigning with Joy and Adopting for Joy, sections four and five, unlock the strategies of leaders flourishing with technology. I'll introduce the eliminate, accelerate, and adopt method I uncovered interviewing entrepreneurs, multidisciplinary artists, CEOs, parents, and joyful creators all around the world. This is where things get especially fun: people who are happy with technology do things differently.

You can think of the sections of the book as the "why" and the chapters as the "how."

Throughout the book, you'll find interactive sidebar questions, where you can reflect on your own journey along the way.

Good Burdens will not teach you how to break up with your phone or pawn off cheap life hacks to prove you can get more things done. Instead, you're going to learn how to stop living life on autopilot and start living a life so wild and good, so brimming with joy, that your screens dim in comparison.

I am going to teach you how to take up good burdens—commitments to people and creative work that shape the beating breathing world—because "genuine love, with all the discipline it requires, is the only path in this life to substantial joy."[4]

A life of passive consumption is not what you were made for.

You were made for more. You were made to love.

It is worth the effort.

> You're going to learn how to stop living life on autopilot, and start living a life so wild and good...that your screens dim in comparison.

I

THE ALGEBRA OF JOY

Q. What is joy?

A. The emotion evoked by well-being, success, or good fortune or by the prospect of possessing what one desires.

One hugely powerful force has gotten in the way of your joy. FOMO.

You know what FOMO is: Fear of Missing Out.

It's one of the most powerful forces of the modern age. There's no question that FOMO won the last decade. A ten-years inferno stoked by attention-grabbing, depression-breeding, bottom-of-the-brain-stem–abusing online platforms, classic advertising slogans (*You are not enough. You don't have enough.*) and Silicon Valley's tech inevitability subterfuge—the lies the tech industry tell themselves, and us: that facial recognition, smart diapers, and surveillance devices are inevitable evolutions, and having them is imperative to our happiness.

Fear of Missing Out won the day.

Don't believe for a moment, though, that FOMO just sprang into being in the last twenty years or so; it's a symptom of some of the most fundamental forces that lie within us as social beings: the desire to belong, to fit in, to know where we are in our tribe.

FOMO is unique. It's part jealousy, part information overload, part insecurity, part anxiety, part low self-image. FOMO is externalizing our joy and using comparison as the main lens through which we judge our own worthiness. FOMO would be powerless if we didn't, on some level, believe that what we choose to do and be, and how we live, are best evaluated by comparing ourselves to everyone we know.

I mentioned that FOMO isn't a new concept, but we *do* have a FOMO epidemic like never before in history. Why? Because of two increasingly powerful forces that act like steroids for FOMO: capitalism and social media. These systems aren't intrinsically sinister, but both are built in a way that makes it incredibly easy for toxic forces like FOMO to become more powerful than ever before. Because at their core, each system invites us to situate ourselves in relation to what we are *lacking*. Both capitalism and profit-driven social media are trying to convince you that the life you have is not good enough.

It's natural to compare ourselves to other humans. We're meant to live in families and communities, to know who we can trust and rely on and for what. We live up to the responsibilities of our jobs and our families by acquiring certain levels of skill and by having a clear picture of how capable we should be to meet those responsibilities. However, our modern condition short-circuits this in a few ways: we're able to know and see more about what other humans are doing—both those we know and those we don't know at all—than at any time in human history. If you lived before social media, as many of us did, the idea of knowing specifically the personal thoughts— whether about a movie, a brand, or a political issue—of thirty thousand random people would have once sounded impossible. Today, we can just read the comments.

Have you heard of Dunbar's number? In the 1990s, British anthropologist Robin Dunbar studied the brains and social groups of various primates, including humans, and compared them. He came to the conclusion that humans are capable of maintaining about 150 *stable human connections*; he defined

What do you imagine makes up a good life?

these as relationships in which one knows who each person is and how they all relate to each other.

How many "friends" do you have on social media? How many people do you see regularly on your commute? In your workplace? In your family? We haven't even counted your in-person friends yet.

The point is this: our brains have not caught up with us; they have not evolved to measure ourselves against the sheer number of vacations, jobs, cars, partners, and waist sizes that we now can. Given the infinite variety of lives being lived, it's inevitable that, with unlimited access, we'll find people who do or have something "better" than us in every single way. That's enough to give anyone FOMO 24/7.

This feeds into our global culture of materialism and capitalism. At its core, the economy is people buying and selling stuff. Simple enough, nothing evil there. But *why* do people buy stuff?

Because they need it, you're probably saying. But what if you've already got everything you really need in a modern society: a home, enough food and clothing, health care, a way to get online, and a way to get where you need to go? What's going to motivate you to buy anything now? Well, you'll also *want* things, you're probably saying. But what happens when you get something you want: treat yourself to a new outfit, phone, or maybe even a car? You need to keep wanting things, or the people who sell things are out of work.

What if you've already got clothes you like, a home you like, a job you like…a life you like? To keep you buying, you need to be kept wanting. And what better way to make you want something you didn't know you wanted than by showing you people, happy, beautiful people whom you've probably never met or even heard of, who have it?

You can see where this is going.

The synergy between our modern technology and our modern economic system is that there's a lot of interest out there in *giving* us FOMO, because FOMO keeps us glued to our devices, keeps us buying, and keeps us hustling in side gigs.

You Are Always Missing Out

If you weren't in Texas last week, you missed out…on a tornado. You missed out on having your house destroyed, and maybe being hurt. At its simplest, missing out simply means that one thing is present when another is absent. The absent thing *should* be something we don't want or need, but too often the things we're missing out on today are things we need most.

After hearing that, you might be saying, "Well, it's not the same thing. I didn't *choose* to miss a tornado. I just wasn't there." The point is that this is happening, organically, every minute of our lives, whether we're choosing it or not. You're missing out on everything but reading right now because you chose to. But you didn't choose to miss out on living in nineteenth-century France. When and where you were born wasn't under your control, but it caused you to miss out on the life experiences of anyone born under any other circumstances.

Somewhere right now, someone you know, maybe even a good friend, appears to be having more fun than you. They're buying something nice that you might not be able to afford. They're getting a job offer for an amazing, fulfilling, well-paid position. They're on their way to a great vacation in an exotic locale.

You're not doing any of those things. How does that make you feel? How does it make you think about the value of what you are doing right now?

This is where the Fear Of Missing Out comes from. The danger of forces like FOMO is not only in the pressure to try to do, be, and experience everything, *it's the lie we're told that it's possible to.* Every moment of your existence is spent doing one thing to the exclusion of a literal infinity of other things. No matter what you choose.

FOMO's core messages:

I'm not *doing* enough.

I don't *have* enough.

I *am* not enough.

If you stopped believing all three of these at once, you'd never again buy something you saw on Instagram, you'd never do another minute of unpaid overtime, you'd never doubt your worthiness to be loved, and a *lot* of people would make a *lot* less money off you.

Simply put, the antidote for FOMO is *joy*.

When was the last time you felt joy?

Are you feeling it right now? Are you feeling it because you're away from your responsibilities? Are you feeling joy because you're in nature? Maybe you're feeling it because you've given yourself permission to rest. Are you feeling it right now because you're excited about what you might learn reading these pages?

When was the last time you felt joy?

Where were you? Who were you with? Were you alone? What did it smell like? What could you hear? What were you doing? What could you see?

Close your eyes and take a moment with that memory.

The Elements of Joy

The experience of joy involves two things: active noticing and nurturing. Noticing is about your attention. Nurturing is about your effort. In the following pages, I am going to show you why I think effortful living is the path to joy and the steps you can take to get there, but we can't talk about any of that without an understanding of what I mean by joy.

Joy isn't necessarily happiness, or comfort, or delight. In fact, some of those things can be obstacles to joy. I've spent a lot of time connecting to people, researching, and talking on the subject, and the bottom line is that joy is experiencing what we all want: well-being and success, however we define them for ourselves. It's written right into the dictionary definition of the word. Success means the attainment of our goals, whatever they are. Well-being is having a positive relationship with our limits and our abilities, whatever they are. Joy occurs when well-being and success exist simultaneously within us. Beating FOMO means defining your success and your well-being and synthesizing them into joy that is uniquely, profoundly, and humanly your own.

> The experience of joy involves two things: active noticing and nurturing. Noticing is about your attention. Nurturing is about your effort.

First Element of Joy: Success

Do you consider yourself successful? If not, why not? If you do consider yourself successful, is your success the source of your joy? Do you need anything else? Why are you reading this book?

The first ingredient in a joyful life is success. And the definition that applies to every human being on the planet is pretty simple: the achievement of goals. The more goals we achieve, the more successful we are. Since success makes up half the equation of joy, we need goals in our life, always, if we want a shot at joy.

So, the real question is: how do we define these goals that will make us experience success?

If you live in a modern, technological, post-industrial society as many of us do, your goals will probably be mostly professional: earn this much money, achieve this title, launch a successful startup. Someone who lives in a small rural village might have different goals, like: wake early for the harvest, attend to the children, be home before dark.

All of these goals have something in common: they're rooted in externalities, things outside ourselves. And that's okay, because most of life is about meeting challenges that arise from outside ourselves. But if we're seeking joy, we need to be aware of *where* those external goals come from, because too often goals are set for us by entities that don't care about our joy or, in the worst cases, need to work directly against our joy in order to profit.

Remember those messages?

You don't have enough. You are not doing enough. You are not enough.

So, where do good goals come from? Behavioural psychologists have long established that the best goals, the ones most likely to be achieved positively, have three common traits: they are specific, measurable, and time-sensitive.

In his raucous book *The Subtle Art of Not Giving a Fuck*, blogger and internet entrepreneur Mark Manson says, "The key to a good life is not giving a fuck about more; it's giving a fuck about less, giving a fuck about only what is true and immediate and important."

Sound familiar?

True: measurable.

Immediate: time-sensitive.

Important: specific.

Today, we have no end of labour-saving technologies and yet we still feel as though we never have enough time. We have wealth unparalleled in human history and yet we work harder than ever for more. Scarcity, the never-enough problem, is rooted in the belief that we *are not* enough, that we *don't have* enough: time, money, success, or whatever it might be.

As shame and vulnerability researcher Dr. Brené Brown says, this feeling of scarcity "does thrive in shame-prone cultures that are steeped in comparison and fractured by disengagement."[5]

So how do you combat scarcity?

You do it with gratitude. Gratitude is the means by which we measure our success. It's about pausing between successes to evaluate where that success came from and then celebrate it.

True Measures of Success

I want to tell you about my friend Rebecca.

She lives in a small house in a working-class neighbourhood in Queens, New York, with her husband, a roommate, two dogs, a cat, a turtle, and a half-dozen chickens. She works as a freelance copywriter, English teacher, and psychotherapist. Rebecca has never earned a six-figure salary in her entire life and isn't likely to ever do so. She has no professional title that will ever mean anything outside the organizations where she works. You will probably never know who she is. But Rebecca considers herself a W-I-L-D success.

Four nights a week, from about seven to midnight, Rebecca's house fills with friends—some of whom she's known for over thirty years. They share meals, play cards and video games, make cocktails, and watch stupid shows on Netflix.

She's been with her husband for over fifteen years and they've weathered a lot of things: mental illness in the family, unemployment, and more.

Rebecca can sustain herself in the wilderness for a month, speak three languages, and cook hundreds of meals—none of which add to her after-tax earnings.

Rebecca has a collection of valued, long-term relationships with people who are intensely, shockingly loyal, and has the soft and hard skills to physically survive just about anywhere in the world.

She has a home she can afford and animals she loves that love her back. She's healthy, feels valued, and never does a moment more work than she wants to.

She's not on Facebook, Instagram, or Twitter.

Rebecca's goals are sustainable, positive, and don't require her to derive her worth outside of herself.

Remember: success is the achievement of goals. It doesn't matter how large or small a goal is. What does "a big goal" even mean? Is making a billion dollars a big goal? Is keeping a relationship for life? Which is bigger?

Setting goals compatible with joy is about choosing them honestly, actively, and with self-awareness.

These elements are crucial; if we're not honest about what we want when we set a goal, we'll fail. *Guaranteed*. And worse yet, it won't be the productive failure everyone's obsessed with these days. It'll be the failure that leads to quitting and despair.

When our goals are disconnected from joy, they won't survive setbacks. They won't survive the inevitable hardships and challenges that come with being alive. They won't last beyond our mood swings, social trends, or cravings.

This leads us to some serious crossroads. Remember, joy is missing out on some things to have others.

Rebecca may never earn six figures, but with a couple of phone calls, she can take the afternoon off and go to an art museum and her work will still be there tomorrow.

For you, missing out might mean having a child instead of accepting a position that would require travel nine months out of the year. Or vice versa. It might mean accepting a lower level of compensation for the ability to do work you love more or do fewer things you call work. Or vice versa. The important element is that the direction you take at the crossroads is chosen honestly, actively, and with self-awareness. These are not easy choices. Joy is not passive. It is something we must actively seek out for ourselves.

Joy is not passive. It is something we must actively seek out for ourselves.

Own your choices. Celebrate them. Be honest with yourself at all times, even if you can't always be honest with the outside world.

Second Element of Joy: Well-Being

When American academic and business consultant Clayton Christensen, the man famous for coining the tech industry's favourite term, "disruption," was asked to address his students at Harvard, he turned it into a short book called *How Will You Measure Your Life?* that spends basically no time at all discussing disruption, market strategies, or innovation—his areas of expertise. Instead, Christensen spends the whole book talking about well-being.

Why? Because well-being is the second element of joy.

The simplicity of this may surprise you. And you may wonder why I'm not using the arguably more popular word, "wellness." Here's why. "Be" is a verb. "Being" describes the active maintenance of a state. Wellness, to me, is a descriptor, like wealth or beauty. You have it or you don't. It's outside of you. If you don't have it, you will probably want it and chase it. I want to challenge you to think of well-being as your relationship to who you are instead of a pursuit of things you may or may not have. Like any relationship to a living thing, it's dynamic, forever in motion. Tending to your well-being is a life-long pursuit.

Back to Christensen. On the last day of class, he would ask his students to answer three questions:

- How can I be sure that I'll be happy in my career?
- How can I be sure that my relationships with my spouse and my family become an enduring source of happiness?
- How can I be sure that I'll stay out of jail?

That last one sounds funny, but it's not. Two of his classmates, including an Enron executive, did go to jail. The true measure of life, that's what Christiansen was after.

What does all this have to do with well-being?

Joy Begins and Ends with Warm Relationships

I want to propose to you today that well-being is rooted, more than anything else in your life, in the quality and intimacy of your relationships. I have the research to back it up, including one of the most important studies of human flourishing, the Harvard Grant Study, which you already heard about in the introduction.

It was the capacity for intimate relationships that predicted flourishing in all aspects of the participants' lives.

I realize this is a radical argument to make, that the bottom line of your well-being is quality relationships, but I mean it. Of course, things like diet, exercise, life balance, having a home, education, and so forth are parts of what makes well-being, but the quality of your relationships is even more fundamental.

Why? Aside from the intrinsic benefit to your physical and mental health, warm relationships facilitate the other parts: the diet, the exercise, the financial security. When we have deep, meaningful, warm relationships, we have people looking out for us and helping us get the things we need. We know it's easier to stick to a fitness program if you have a friend keeping you accountable. We know it's easier to find a good job or get into a good school with friends who can refer, recommend, and advocate for you.

Likewise, you're motivated to do the same: to support and care for the people on the other end of those bonds, which empowers, motivates, and energizes you. One flows into the other.

It all begins with warm relationships.

Let me give you a great example.

Arax and I met at the rowing club. She was looking for a partner and so was I. I could tell there was a significant age spread, but we both wanted to row recreationally, so it was a good fit. It turns out Arax was a lot more hard-core than I was. One day, a couple of miles into our morning workout, I managed to pipe out: "Arax, how old are you anyway?" It turned out she was sixtysomething to my thirtysomething years old. The white hair should have given it away.

Arax had a habit of calling me "Mighty Christina," which just made me feel so powerful and capable inside. I loved hearing about her varied and exciting life. She had designed clothing for rowers, was an international liaison for a university, and had even worked for the United Nations. She'd had so much life experience.

One day we flipped our boat, which happens, and it can go one of two ways: it can bring out the worst in people, like any crisis, or it can bring out the best. In this case, we just laughed our asses off, swam ourselves back to shore, dumped out the boat, and rowed back to the club looking like two drowned rats.

I enjoyed regularly spending time with someone so far outside my regular peer group, someone older than I was, and that we had so much fun together. I loved the connection to the water, seeing the sunrise, the smell of the morning air, and the wildlife. I loved pushing my body and my mind to focus on the momentum and swing of the boat. All of these things supported me *being* well.

It would have been easy to stop rowing. Paying my club dues, getting up at 5:30 A.M. to leave my sleeping family, driving to the docks to hoist a boat overhead and wait in line to launch: these are all reasons I could have stopped. But it was the social bond and the connection to nature intrinsic to the sport that kept me coming back.

That's what I'm trying to tell you about how well-being actually works. The most successful people, the ones whom Christensen told his students to emulate and the ones who flourished in the Grant Study, started with well-being, and success came as a consequence. When I partnered with Arax, I wanted to have fun, be outdoors, and connect to someone. Physical fitness, confidence, and self-discipline came as a consequence.

Pursue warm relationships, and the rest will follow. Commit yourself to people who have committed themselves to you. It's the only way you can expect the long-term dividends that the most successful subjects of the Grant study experienced.

Attention is the Beginning of Devotion

Conversely? If you don't have this, it's pretty bad.

The average person in the United States has only one close friend, according to the *American Sociological Review*.[6] One in four people has no confidantes—meaning simply a close friend they can confide in—at all. *Zero*. To make things worse, 75 percent of people say they are unsatisfied with the friendships they do have. Meanwhile, religious service attendance and other traditional means of in-person gathering are in decline. New ways of gathering in the real world can be hard to find.

This level of disconnection is dangerous to our health. Chronic loneliness has been alleged to have the same impact on our life expectancy as smoking fifteen cigarettes a day, with a risk factor that rivals excessive drinking or obesity. It's common sense that things like smoking and poor diet are bad for us: why is it so hard for us to understand that loneliness is just as real, and just as deadly?

How do we end up being deprived, depriving ourselves, of this lifeblood that the most intelligent people have concluded makes our existence healthier, longer, and better?

Chasing other things, for one.

We tend to imagine that if we pursue and accumulate the short-term rewards our society has set up for us, primarily wealth and material goods, we can deal with the touchy-feely stuff later. *Maybe* in retirement. *Maybe* when we've made so much money or gotten so far in our careers that we feel we can throttle back. But experience shows that we don't.

It's easy for me to get caught up in my revolving roles: wife, mother of three, daughter, creative entrepreneur, neighbour, friend. The sheer overwhelm of an average day can make it difficult to see the forest for the trees: the community of care I've chosen to be a part of and the creative contributions I've chosen to make; *the purpose of it all*. Do you feel that way, too?

In studying success and successful people, Clayton Christensen saw people think this way:

[people] tell themselves that they could divide their lives into stages, spending the first part pushing forward in their careers, and imagining that at some future point they would spend time with their families—only to find that by then their families were gone.

Reflect on your own roles. How much energy do you give to each of them?

One of my favourite poets, Mary Oliver, believes that *attention is the beginning of devotion*. Much like you, my attention is pulled in a hundred different directions a day: toward my children and endless household tasks. Toward creative projects and bills to pay. In short, it's spread thin.

It was clear the day my husband and I walked into a new therapist's office that the most vital relationship in our lives, our marriage, warranted extra attention.

After our therapy appointment, we picked our kids up from a smattering of houses around the neighbourhood. Once home, I texted our friends to thank them for their support. One mother wrote back to say:

I feel honored that you trust us and I am happy to be able to play any role in helping you find the time to work on your marriage. Marriage requires such constant

When you imagine a good life now, what do you see? What are your good burdens?

attention and devotion, doesn't it? And with young children, it's difficult to carve out the necessary time. We are always here when you need us, that's what a community is for. Xo

That was the moment I let myself cry—for us, for terrible things we'd said and done, for our three children. How our love made them. How our broken love birthed inexplicable hope.

Love. Passion. Quiet. Pain. These are the folds of our knownness. Our bodies a map. Each scar, a city. Each tear, a lake. Every laugh, a mountain. Every child, a continent.

Years of laughter. Years of terrible things. Hope, our compass.

Yes, our most essential relationships require constant attention and devotion. We don't live or love well in rushing. We can only love so many people well.

My marriage is a good burden.

Choosing Your Joy

I started this section by asking, when was the last time you felt joy? Now, think about when the next time will be, because it is in your own hands. I hope you see that. I hope you've seen how we've been fed a lie about where a good life comes from, usually by people with an interest in offering us access to it on their terms, and often at an invisible, terrible price.

I hope you've seen how your success isn't externally defined—by a dollar amount, a title, units shipped, hours logged, miles run—but by achieving the goals you've set for yourself, which may include those things, or not.

Real goals are yours, starting from inside you, and they happen when you tell yourself honestly what brings you joy.

I hope you've seen how wonderfully, simply, well-being is rooted in cultivating and maintaining warm relationships with friends, family, partners, neighbours. Anyone worthy of the time you choose to spend, who affirm you, raise you up, and with whom you can give and receive love.

I hope you've seen how, when you fill your life with quality relationships, the other elements of physical, mental, and emotional health will flow more naturally and smoothly.

In the next two sections, Discovering Your Joys and Being Led by Joy, you will begin unlocking what makes you *you*; the unique community of care you want to commit to, the creative contributions you want to make, and the relationships that will support you along the way.

Be Here

Mindfulness is a tool of resistance. In the attention economy, mental clarity has become a subversive act.
—Jay Vidyarthi

I once attended a talk by Zen monk Haemin Sunim, author of the global bestselling book *The Things You Can See Only When You Slow Down*. Getting there wasn't slow—travelling at death-defying speeds through the streets of London in the back of a classic black cab—but once I was inside the quiet space of Saint Stephen's Hall, I could feel my pulse slow. Someone handed me a gin and tonic in a teacup. *How blissfully British*. I asked two well-dressed women if I could sneak a seat beside them and we struck up a conversation immediately. Introductions were made from the small stage at the front of the room and a conversation between Haemin and *Idler* magazine editor Tom Hodgkinson began.

Haemin shared wonderfully simple advice on how to slow down and find meaning in our day-to-day lives, such as going out of your way to meet a loved one at the bus stop or picking your children up from school. (Remember how it felt to see your mother's face after a full day of kindergarten?) Loving, intentional acts. Hearing Haemin speak affirmed the choices I'd been making at home and at work, to prioritize deeper connections, joy, meaning, and rest—away from the tyranny of the urgent.

After the event, I found myself making more of an effort to put away my phone, to allow myself to daydream, trust my own ideas, and enjoy idle time alone and with loved ones.

I've fallen in love with this magazine, *Idler*. I picked up my first copy on that trip but didn't get around to reading it until eight months later. The theme of the issue? *Procrastination*.

I don't know about you, but I am so tempted to speed: to do more, to feed my ego, to keep up with the Joneses. But it's true, what Haemin says: there are many things you can only see—and create—when you slow down. I want to pursue this discipline and joy. I long to create good work and nurture loving relationships—fruit that will last.

Near the end of the evening, Haemin led us in a simple meditation for ourselves, for the strangers whose hands we held in the room, and for two people who were not present. I chose my children:

> *May you be happy.*
> *May you be healthy.*
> *May you be peaceful.*
> *May you be protected.*
> *May you always be protected.*

We repeated the meditation slowly, many times. Over and over. *Happy. Healthy. Peaceful. Protected. Always protected.*

Power of Presence

The Dutch have a word for the art of being together for no purpose: *niksen*. Niksen can help us become people who are generous by teaching the value of being together with no desired outcome at all. Instead of constantly occupying your mind with what to do next or bouncing from one task to another, niksen is the practice of mindful idleness. Niksen is about slowing it all down. Niksen is about saying, *The world will keep turning without me. I'm not the centre of the universe. That's okay.*

In what parts of your life have you let media come between yourself and others?

Niksen is about the power of presence.

The inability to be present to your experience has a lot do with your phone. Just the physical presence of a phone has proven to negatively affect how we relate to others. People who carry on a conversation with a cellphone simply present in the room feel their relationship quality worsens. On the flip side, interacting without a cellphone nearby seems to help foster closeness, connectedness, interpersonal trust, and perceptions of empathy: the building blocks of relationship.

The impact of screens on your ability to be present and build closeness takes on a new valence when you think about those whose love you desire most.

Living in Between

The average person spends 145 minutes on social media per day.[7]

It was a pivotal moment the day my friend Steven, a lawyer and two-time tech founder in Toronto, realized he spent more time checking his new wife's Instagram account than he did talking to her on a daily basis. Their daily hustle to get their respective businesses off the ground left these two effervescent extroverts with little time or energy for intimacy at the end of their day.

Media, by definition, means in between. Where in your life have you settled for less, letting media take the place of real relationship?

"If you're going to do it, be there for it," implores social psychology professor Dr. Ellen Langer, the world's pre-eminent mindfulness expert. The first tenured woman in Harvard's psychology department, Langer began studying mindfulness during the 1970s, discovering early on that attention is directly related to well-being.

When I reach out to Dr. Langer to talk about what she means when she says, "when we make the moment matter, it all matters," she tells me she doesn't like my line of questioning and

If you're going to do it, be there for it.

demands a straight shot at talking about our experience of the global pandemic. I like a woman who knows what she wants, so I let her rip:

"I think what people need to understand is that all we have is moments and all of our stress is based on the future," she says. "People should be aware now, if they weren't before, that the future is unpredictable. People are stressed because they think of things as unpredictable now, but *things were always unpredictable* and so people tend to confuse the stability of their mind-sets, what they're thinking, with what's actually happening. Everything has always been changing.

"Interestingly," adds Dr. Langer, "when we look back, everything makes sense, you know?"

She gives the example of a hypothetical couple named Jane and Joe. Let's say you discover they're getting divorced. You say to yourself, *Yeah, I knew that,* because you start thinking of the fight they had at a party and how rude they were to each other the last time you saw them. If somebody said at the party, "Well, do you think they're going to get divorced?" You would have probably said, "No, everybody fights."

This is an example of how we can fuse the certainty of things: all that's already happened with the uncertainty going forward. Hindsight is 20/20.

Dr. Langer does an exercise with her advanced Decision Making and the Psychology of Possibility class at Harvard. The students start off like most people, believing that everything is predictable. So Ellen says to them: "Okay, I've been teaching a version of this for forty years. I have never missed a class. What is the likelihood that I'm going to be here next week?" She then goes around the room and everybody answers, and they say things like 98 percent; it's as if they know they shouldn't say a hundred, but essentially that's what they're saying.

Then she asks her students to give her a good reason why she might not be there next week.

The first person invariably says Dr. Langer is always there so she might not be in class because she deserves the time off. The next person says Dr. Langer might miss class because she has to take her dog to the vet. They all give very Harvard-worthy answers before she asks them the question again: "Now, what do you think the likelihood is of my being here next week?"

At this point, 99 percent drops to 50 percent.

In times of unrest and change, it's important to realize that the certainty we thought we had wasn't ever real.

The point Dr. Langer is trying to make is that in times of unrest and change, it's important to realize that the certainty we thought we had wasn't ever real, so that we become more comfortable with uncertainty.

Things will play out however they play out.

It will seem that there are advantages and disadvantages for all of us. But Dr. Langer insists that these perceived opportunities or setbacks aren't real. *They're a function of the way we frame an event.* Your experience of events depends on the way you frame them, the narrative you tell about yourself, which means that your stress is essentially of your own making. This is imperative to understand, particularly for those of us who are extremely anxious, frustrated, or overwhelmed.

Stress relies on two things, she explains. First, something is going to happen. Second, when it happens, we believe it's going to be awful. But, as we've already established, we don't know what's going to happen.

"So, if you think about two, four, or six reasons why the terrible thing we think might happen won't happen, we already feel better," she explains.

This is how mindfulness—active noticing—reduces stress. With it, we have a chance at seeing things as they really are.

Ellen Langer's best advice: *Just take care of right now.* When you're mindful, you're there for it, so whatever's happening you will be able to take advantage of opportunities you might not otherwise have known were even available to you.

In my friend Steven's case, a baby was on its way and he wanted to make a change. The first step was deleting Instagram off his phone to nudge him to reach out his hand and ask his partner about her day.

The Bat Cave on the Shelf

One day, Aaron Reynolds noticed a LEGO set he'd begun with his son was gathering dust. That year, he'd allowed numerous creative projects and significant work travel to consume his time. He wanted a change.

> I got the 1960s Batcave for Christmas and finished building it about a year later because it sat in a box for seven or eight months because there just wasn't time. When I began evaluating all of the pressures on my time, wanting to have a more normal life with good quality time with my kids, my wife and my friends, I realized I needed to get back at least 20 or 30 hours a week that I was putting into "stuff."

As the self-employed founder of a number of massive social media accounts, including the wildly popular Effin' Birds, Aaron considers himself "very online." It wasn't always serving him well. He explains: "I wake up in the morning. I read all of my replies. I schedule times throughout the day to check the news so I am able to react to how people are feeling in the world. I am trying to be less online while still being online enough to do the things I need to do. That's hard sometimes. Notifications are the devil and I work hard to have relevant ones."

To reclaim such a significant amount of time a week, Aaron had to make big changes.

Around the same time, he began leaving his headphones at home when he commuted, because he realized he wasn't spending enough time with his own thoughts.

> Every part of my commute or walking used to be spent listening to an audiobook or a podcast or music. I realized I need a little more space for my brain to breathe, a time where I'm not evaluating a second stimulus on top of what's happening around me. That's been really good for me. I only realized that I needed it after forgetting my headphones one day.

"When we're frazzled, our fight-or-flight response is on overload, causing a host of problems," says clinical health psychologist Dr. Amy Sullivan.[8] "We can use calm, quiet moments to tap into a different part of the nervous system that helps shut down our bodies' physical response to stress." Being still and silent can help you lower your blood pressure, decrease your heart rate, steady your breathing, and increase focus and cognition.

> When it comes to your use of technology, it's always a work in progress. You've got to keep thinking about it. Technology—all of these things—are what we make of it. If you are scrolling Twitter and getting nothing from

it then why are you doing it, you know? And if you are having an argument with someone online and are you are getting nothing from it, why are you doing it? You have to find your balance and your benefit.

When we wear headphones all day, we might miss profound thoughts, moments of connection, and vital decompression. In order to make a more joyful life, you need to *be here*.

(Surprise! FOMO is really about *not being present*.)

Your presence is the greatest gift you have to offer others. This fleeting experience that will pass in a moment? You will show up for it, you will be there, and then it will be gone. And that moment will have meant something because of *you*, because you gave your whole self to it.

Don't miss it.

Oh, and the Batcave? It's finished now.

Let us be the ones who live for today;
who savour our experiences.

Quests

1. Plan one hour of niksen (mindful idle time with a loved one) this week.

2. The next time you go out, leave your headphones at home. Notice what you notice.

3. Recite this short mindfulness meditation, first for yourself and again for a loved one:

May you be happy.
May you be healthy.
May you be peaceful.
May you be protected.
May you always be protected.

Take up the good burden of being here.

Be Awake

Be careful not to sleepwalk through the only life you have.
Wake up. Blink hard. Stretch. Keep moving.
—Maggie Smith, poet

Happy was the day I discovered saint, composer, and poet Hildegard of Bingen, who believed that the only failure in life is to not take delight in the beauty and grace of creation. "The only sin is drying up," she wrote. "Do whatever it takes to get wet and green, moist and juicy."

Well, then. That's my kind of nun.

"Wake up," she said.

So, I did.

Hiding Out

There was once a time, before you were born, when the only problems people heard about were within their own tribe, or maybe the tribe next door. If you heard about the problem, you probably could do something to help.

You know nothing of that world. You know only a reality where it is possible to hear about every terrible thing happening on the globe in real time. This is overwhelming to the point where you feel there's nothing you can do about it. Talk about *stress*.

You probably don't always cry about the terrible things you hear about either. If you did, you'd never stop. You can't cry about all of the things, so you cry about none of the things.

Instead of feeling sad and moved to action, you are exhausted and worried. You know this. Anxiety has sky-rocketed over the same time period. You feel the fear. It is a state of being.

"How can we walk, and run, and live and laugh, when we can't count on the ground beneath us?" asks Dave Eggers in his beautiful children's book *The Lifters*, which follows a young boy and girl using found objects— mops, umbrellas, hockey sticks— to try and prop up a town collapsing in despair.

The breathless pace of the internet has led a lot of us into hiding. The reason you're easily distractable is not because you have a self-control problem, but because you feel you can't meet the exhausting expectations of our modern world. You *want* an escape route.

I have known too many days I could not bear the burden of being in the world, and willfully checked out.

My neighbour told me her boss keeps asking her how she's doing. "I don't want to stop long enough to answer that question," she confessed from her paint-chipped front porch.

I get it. I have known too many days I could not bear the burden of being in the world, and willfully checked out.

I remember when I started hiding. It happened quite slowly, really. A glacial-paced abandonment of self. Maybe you know what I'm talking about.

We'd moved across country, from Vancouver to Toronto, the year before. It took just one cross-continental flight to shift a lifetime of rich relationships onto the internet. In short time, "staying in touch" looked like scrolling through people's posts. The time difference was no longer a problem, because I could scroll at my convenience, any time, day or night. The only problem was that a few of my closest family members were nowhere online, and my contact with them all but evaporated. I was gleaning information and little else.

In Tristan Harris's words: I was forgetting.[9]

Harris, a former Google insider who has grown in celebrity by publicly questioning how technology affects us, told *Wired* magazine: "When you use technology, you have goals. When you land on YouTube, it doesn't know any of those goals. It has one goal, which is to make you forget those goals that you have."

To understand why we continue choosing apps and platforms designed to addict us, we need only consider our tidy online profiles, the ease of mobile ordering, and the soothing voice-activation of Alexa. Each of these time-saving applications serves our predilection, fulfilling technology's promise to get everything under control and increase productivity with as little difficulty as possible. They're the path of least resistance in an already full and often volatile life. Apple, Google, Amazon, and Facebook are more than willing to pave the way for our convenience in return for our time and attention.

Writer Tim Wu calls it "the tyranny of convenience."[10]

"Today's cult of convenience fails to acknowledge that difficulty is a constitutive feature of human experience." Making things easier isn't wicked, Wu argues, but the promise of "smooth, effortless efficiency...threatens to erase the sort of struggles and challenges that help give meaning to life. Created to free us, it can become a constraint on what we are willing to do, and thus in a subtle way it can enslave us."

The more time I spent online, the more disconnected I felt from the real world, which sent me deeper down the rabbit hole. *Much deeper.*

> *Acedia* (noun) Spiritual or mental sloth; apathy. Origin: early 17th century: late Latin, from Greek akēdia 'listlessness,' from a- **'without'** + kēdos **'care.'**

Seeing this word for the first time but not versed in its meaning, I felt it knew me already. Meaningless, meaningless. It's all meaningless. I turn back into and over the Ecclesiastical lines: *There is nothing new under the sun.* Why try? Why write? It's all been said before.

Our online environments—where we now spend the lion's share of our waking hours—can be controlled, while the natural world and the human experience are intrinsically unpredictable. A meaningful life may offer a mix of suffering and joy. It's a painful way, filled with many unknowns, much disorder, and assured valleys along with mountaintops. It's a way of trust. That's why, once we've tasted the pleasures of convenience and control, it's difficult to turn away.

> *Listless* (of a person or their manner) lacking energy or enthusiasm: bouts of listless depression. Origin: Middle English: from obsolete **list** 'appetite, desire' + **-less**.

I hate how hard I find it to be alive, how easy it seems for others.

Please understand that the only reason I can speak with any authority about hiding out from the real world is because I have known that void so intimately.

I began my journey back the day I spoke my despair out loud to my friend Amanda:

> *One day we will walk shoulder to shoulder around the seawall and talk for hours about the ways our lives have folded and unfolded these past ten years. That day will come. I can see it. I can taste it. I can't wait for it. I will tell you about how for five years I travelled further and further inward and the way some gentle spirit patiently coaxed me outward again. I will tell you about the felt CC badge my nine-year-old friend Clara lovingly hand-sewed for my birthday and that I now carry in my back pocket as if it's laden with superpowers (it is).*

I will tell you about marriage and depression. The jet-lag-induced fight Michael and I had in a damp stairwell steps away from Trafalgar Square. How our children, oscillating between terror and indifference, picked stones up off the ground as our voices rose and fell. How the people stopped and stared at us. How our daughter screamed.

I'll tell you about anxiety and learning that laziness is non-love and that there's a thing called learned helplessness (holy hell) and I had it bad for a thousand reasons but one day got sick of pretending I didn't know what I was doing.

And I will ask you about your new superpowers and far-off dreams and demand you take me to the new Vancouver haunt that's the best thing since sliced bread and stay there talking with you about all the things until they kick us out the door. That day is coming.

Until then, I look forward to seeing your beautiful face again soon through the power of Zoom and count my blessings this technology exists.

Speaking this despair out loud released an inner valve. Amanda bore witness to my suffering and reached out a hand. A chord of care was extended, and, with it, I was being woven back into community.

Reclaiming the Real

Over time, I became discontented with this voyeuristic approach to relationships I had developed, but had more or less made peace with it. Until one fateful day. I logged onto social media after having been away for a few days and saw a message on my wall. My friend was in town! She was asking to meet up! My heart swelled with excitement at the prospect of seeing her. I checked the date stamp on the message. It was four days old. I had missed my friend.

It took a full day for the emotions to cycle through me: excitement followed by disappointment followed by frustration, then anger. *Why didn't she put in some effort to email me directly? Why didn't she call? Did she even want to see me?*

Slowly, realization washed over me. I'd been ditching people I'd claimed were important to me for more than a year. I'd allowed the same roundabout communication routes to sneak into my own life. Blaming my friend or the online platform didn't cut it.

That day, I promised myself I would start connecting as directly as possible with the people in my life. It set me on a journey to unfriend convenience in an effort to better serve my loved ones and, ultimately, my own heart.

To get where you want to go, you need to take up the good burden of reality.

Here's how I learned to live awake: by deepening my attachment to and love for the beating, breathing world. By taking up the good burden of the real.

To get where you want to go, you need to take up the good burden of reality. It's the only way I know.

I began to see how, over time, attention enlivens and distraction deadens.

Awake	*Asleep*
Attentive	*Distracted*
Life-Giving	*Life-Taking*
Off Autopilot	*On Autopilot*
Mindful	*Mindless*
Effortful	*Lazy*
Creative	*Consumptive*
Real	*Unreal*

What else would you add to this list?

Waking Up

Why are you here? What else could you be doing right now? For some reason, at this moment, you've chosen to give your full attention to this book. Is it to put something into your life that you're missing? A person or people? Maybe a part of you? Perhaps just the feeling of joy.

At the close of last decade, I spent a slow afternoon experiencing *Age of You*, a vast collection of photography, sculpture, video, and text, at Toronto's Museum of Contemporary Art. In one immersive experience, artists sought to make sense of the great global shifts we've undergone as our world has been furiously reshaped by digital technology—more often for the better, but sometimes for the worse.

It brought into view how every part of our lives has been transformed, disrupted, or made obsolete, including our relationships with ourselves—*our own knowing*—and our need for one another. It showed how in almost every online context, our attention has been in service of someone else, someone who stood to gain by us consuming more information, more products, more connections, and more likes, while, out of sight, they consumed more and more of our data.

The curators, which included Douglas Coupland, the novelist, visual artist, and designer who became the

Create your own list of attention and distraction here. What do they look like? How to they feel?

voice of a generation with his novel *Generation X*, intended to urge viewers to consider how digital capitalism—that is, capitalism conducted through the internet—has forced the self to become more *extreme*. By that, I mean a performance, inauthentic in its portrayal. Just look at TikTok. When it comes to views, spectacle beats substance every time.

When you start looking, you see signs of the extreme all around you.

Extreme fear of what's happening to your personal data. Extreme presentations of self in service of online follower growth. Extreme political polarization. Extreme dis-ease in relationships and communities, online and off, as the lines between the real and unreal—through AI, deep fakes, and fake news—blur beyond recognition.

I finger the ticket stub stapled in my black leather journal.

Museum of Contemporary Art, Toronto, Canada

Daily Admission
December 26

Ticket Price: 10.00
This is your ticket. Final sale – no refunds/exchanges

Proof: This is real.

In 2019, the Pew Research Center found that over half of Americans (54 percent) either got their news "sometimes" or "often" from social media.[11] What is most concerning about this trend is that many users of social media are unable to differentiate between authentic, verifiable information and what is now being called "fake news."

Thomas Jefferson famously said, "Information is the currency of democracy." The available information and the rate of engagement on social media are having a real-world impact that cannot be ignored.

"The breakdown of consensus-based reality is perhaps one of the most dangerous threats there has ever been to our shared human experience. We're not built for so much change so quickly. Technology has outrun our ability to absorb it. Is there any turning back?" the *Age of You* artists asked.

I believe there is. It's why I wrote this book.

What Do You Pay When You Pay Attention?

In his breathtaking book *Stand Out of Our Light*, James Williams deftly asks: what do we really pay when we pay attention?

"You pay with all of the things you could have attended to but didn't: all of the goals you didn't pursue, all of the actions you didn't take, and all of the possible yous you could have been, had you attended to those other things."

Let's do a little math exercise. Instead of spending the 118 minutes you likely spend on social media a day, you could, over the course of a lifetime:

> *Go to the moon and back 32 times*
> *Watch* The Simpsons *series 21.5 times #goals*
> *Climb Mount Everest 32 times*
> *Run 10,000 marathons*
> *Walk your dog 93,000 times*

Instead of doing any of those things, though, you're stuck scrolling on your phone in service of capitalist corporate agendas you know little about. Distractions keep you from doing what you want to do, being who you want to be, wanting what you want to want.

What do you pay when you pay attention? You pay with all of the lives you could have lived.

You're here because you want something.

You're here because you want something.

My friend Sarah Selecky, a novelist and writing coach, often reminds me that to create something new—anything at all—you must trust what seems random. You must let go of control. You must keep time and space for creating, for wanting. For to create is to *want*.

I believe the world will be better with what you want, the things you long to create: your words, your family, your sketches, your inventions, your relationship, your community garden, your charity, your paper dolls, your whatever. To get your ideas down and moving will require your desire. It will require focus. It will require discipline, space, and trust.

It will require you to miss out on some things.

> *Binge-watching*
> *Self-criticism*
> *Impulse pen-shopping on Amazon*
> *The Cut*

If you want to hit your goal, don't scatter your shots.
You're here because you want something. Unpack that want.

> *What is it you want to say?*
> *What do you want to make?*
> *What do you want your family, neighbourhood, work to look like?*
> *What's in you begging—wanting—to come out?*
> *Why—after all—are you here if not because you want something?*

I wrote my first book, *The Joy of Missing Out*, when my children were ages four, two, and six months old. I wrote three days a week from a neighbour's jewellery studio at a desk I rented for twenty-five dollars week. I drove home at lunchtime to nurse and kiss babies. I voice-dictated chapters in the blackness of our bedroom. I wanted to write that book. I was paying for childcare and office space and espresso to make that dream live.

I wanted.

What do you want? And what are you willing to miss out on to get there?

> *Push notifications?*
> *Instagram?*
> *Email?*
> *Lattes?*
> *Holidays?*
> *Expectations—real or imagined?*
> *Alcohol?*
> *Sleep?*
> *Fear?*

I spent four days writing some of this book in the country at a dirty table in a cold room, and I wept for every hour I sat there and gave myself over to the work. This is the work I am meant to do. Those days at that dirty table looked nothing like the front covers and blog posts and productivity hacks and inspirational videos I nibble on and spit out day after day, hour after hour.

The words sprouted and took root. There was nothing productive or Instagrammable or repeatable about it.

I simply made room.

I made room for making. For creating the world I imagined. Cut off the distractions. Left space for what seemed random. Committed to the effort. Stayed in the chair.

Joy happens in the moments when time stops.

It was joy. I know it was joy, because time stopped when I was writing. Joy happens in the moments when time stops.

Time stops when I stay in the chair, trusting what seems random but what is also true. Time stops when I am in the living room, reading poetry aloud to my six-year-old son. Time stops when all about me swirls the world and I sit down.

Where does time stop for you?

Wake up. Notice it—that's when you're experiencing the joy of missing out.

The Way Forward

The beginning of this decade was a nightmare and crucible. It showed us what is essential and non-essential in our lives. Now is the opportunity to ask yourself: what will I carry forward with me? What will I leave behind?

The painful thing about what I am about to say is that you can't move toward joy without wanting. Wanting will get you where you want to go. Trouble is, you may have stopped wanting, ceased willing, abandoned hope. *The world is too broken. Let's shoot for the moon and start over.*

Here's the thing: you might not want to be energized. You might not want to feel joy. You might prefer the comfort of your controlled environment. You might want to feel helpless. You might not want to rock the boat. You might not want to want.

Be honest: what do you want?

There is no middle ground.

You have to choose.

But once you've chosen, there's no turning back.

As Adrienne Rich writes, "The difference between a life lived actively, and a life of passive drifting and dispersal of energies, is an immense difference. Once we begin to feel committed to our lives, responsible to ourselves, we can never again be satisfied with the old, passive way."

Never.

The goal is aliveness. The purpose is love.

Let us be the ones who know true riches;
who value human connection, what is truly real, above all.

Quests

1. Go out and look up at the sky. Witness the white billows edging out the blue. Show someone.

2. Make your own commitment to live awake.

3. Write a list of what you'll give up to make it so.

The goal is aliveness.
The purpose is love.

Take up the good burden of being awake.

II

DISCOVERING YOUR JOYS

A man's true delight is to do the things he was made for.
—Marcus Aurelius, *Meditations*

On a late afternoon walk with my children, we discover a barefoot man making enormous bubbles in the sunshine. The kids beeline for him, and together we spend the better part of an hour darting across fields and park pathways popping hundreds of glittering orbs. A bucket of soapy water, a stick, and a string are all this young man needs to enrapture a crowd of the young and young-at-heart.

As I watch him, I find myself wondering: How old are you? How are you free to spend a weekday afternoon blowing bubbles? What made you so playful?

Bubble man is wearing a black T-shirt with a Holy Mary silkscreened on the front, her upturned lips ceding consent. *Let the children come to me.* He has an open, youthful face. Laughs easily. Leaves a hat out for anyone who feels like tossing a coin in. Never mentions it though. Never minds it. Minds his bubbles and the children and the grass between his toes. Minds the delicious March sunshine.

Marcus Aurelius wrote that a person's true delight is to do the things they were made for.

Delight. Joy. This impulse may give some insight into why, under duress in 2020, the world took up bread baking. As the cast of the Broadway musical *Come from Away* sings: "I need something to do 'cause I can't watch the news." We, too, sought out creative contributions to make meaning in the midst of global upheaval.

We learned to play instruments. Zoomed loved ones. Baked sourdough. Checked on neighbours.

We began noticing and nurturing the things that bring us joy. I asked readers, friends, and members of my digital well-being program, *Navigate*, what brought them joy. Here's what they told me:

- Looking back through old journals
- Being generous
- Cuddling
- Laughing with family
- Tulips
- Reading aloud to loved ones
- Candles burning
- Following through on promises
- Reading stories of endurance
- Getting dressed up
- Playing chess
- Asking for help
- Blanket forts
- Walks in the neighbourhood
- Learning something new
- Playing piano
- Biking
- Hikes in the woods
- Jogging
- Organizing things
- Getting things done
- Colours
- Linear abstract art with nonlinear explanations
- Hip hop beats
- When friends understand
- Writing
- Limiting my choices
- Waking up early
- Making progress toward goals

- Determination
- Confetti
- Turquoise
- Sending and receiving snail mail
- Stamps
- Typewriting
- Helping others
- Receiving words of encouragement
- Deep work
- Flow
- Freedom of the email auto-responder
- Pretty pens
- Being fully alive
- Connecting with friends
- Making things
- Spending time with kids
- Singing
- Marriage
- Cooking
- Cats
- Fires
- Engaging with nature
- Songwriting
- Silence
- Learning
- Musicals
- Dogs
- Spending time out in nature, rain or shine
- Teaching swimming

- Being with family
- Watching baking shows and making our own at home
- Snow
- Shovelling snow
- The ocean
- Poetry
- Felting
- The feel of feet buried in sand
- Sunrises
- Sunsets
- Rowing
- Church
- Barbecues
- Lake swimming
- Camping
- Handwritten notes
- Stickers
- Good tunes
- Live music
- Growing things
- Making new friends
- Overtipping
- Mending things
- Treasure hunts
- Lying under the stars
- Swimming with phosphorescence
- Swings
- Carrot cake
- Swing dancing

- Forgiving others
- Being forgiven
- Hammocks
- Collecting
- Building things
- Being economical
- Letting things go
- Little free libraries
- Tapir .gifs
- Road trips
- Being with brothers and sisters
- *Zoolander*
- Long walks and deep conversation with a friend
- Gardening
- Live events
- Fishing
- Mailing letters
- Going slow
- Kayaking

If you lost count, there were more than one hundred. Say it out loud: One. Hundred. Joys. Isn't that a beautiful sound? Now, let's make a list of your own.

Turn to page 166 and write down ten things that bring you joy *right now*.

Don't skip this step. You'll see why later.

I'll wait.

Now, look back at your list. What do you notice about your joys? Are there any commonalities? How many are about people? About your relationship with yourself? Animals? Objects? Experiences? How many are about movement or the natural world?

Here's what I discovered after years of studying the relationships between technology and joy:

1. Your joys are offline, though technology can help you connect to them.

2. Your joys are connected to your attention and your effort.

3. You can find joy in hard things.

Let's explore.

Defining Your Joy

Discovering what you love is one of the greatest joys and, though you might not have known it, you've been doing it all your life.

Lying in a field as a child and noticing tiny bright buds drawing themselves forward and backward with the wind. *I love buttercup yellow.*

Exploring the world of love in your adolescence. *I love boys who make me laugh.*

Choosing a career path with integrity—true to your desires. *I love helping people.*

Trying your hand at weeding and planting on your friend's farm. *I love whole days spent kneeling in the soil.*

No one else can define your joy. You can and must discover your joys for yourself if you want to know what you were made for.

Not sure what your joys are? Here's an action plan, a simple one. It's rooted in a centuries-old contemplative practice, and one of the reasons I know it's such an effective tool for well-being is that it's been renamed, repackaged, and repeated with its essential function left intact countless times. It originated more than four hundred years ago as the Examen of Consciousness by Saint Ignatius of Loyola, founder of the Jesuits, and has been called "moving toward and away" by motivational psychologists, "energizing and de-energizing habits" by even more motivational psychologists, "life-giving and life-taking practices" by spiritually centred leadership and relationship experts...and I call it *pursuing joy versus despair.*

Whatever you call it, whatever philosophical tradition you're rooting it in, my action plan is an essential resource you can carry with you every day, helping you choose what to do next and discern the right way to go—toward joy.

Here it is.

Tonight, and every night, before you go to sleep, ask yourself these two questions:

> *What was the most life-giving experience of my day?*
> *What was the most life-taking experience of my day?*

Not yesterday, not when you were a kid, not what you're worried about tomorrow, but today. You can use whatever language you wish to describe this: I use *life-giving* and *life-taking*, but you can say joyful vs. despairing, energizing vs. de-energizing.

However you name it, you are actively separating your experiences into things that, if repeated, if pursued, will move you toward joy, as well as those actions that will move you away from it. And so the hardest part of moving forward, deciding the right thing to do, has already been done. What do you want? You want joy, and in the last chapter you already began the process of discovering what your joys, your good burdens, are: the unique experiences, relationships, and things you want more of in your life.

If you asked yourself these questions tonight, what might your answers be? Maybe your most life-giving experience today was holding your partner's hand as you walked down the street, and your most life-taking was agreeing to a totally voluntary activity that you really didn't want to do.

These realizations are valuable. They are how you honestly, actively, and with greater self-awareness admit fundamental truths to yourself about what will lead you toward a more joyful life.

In this case, maybe those truths are these:

> *I want more simple intimacy with my partner.*
> *I want to learn how to say no.*

What happens then? You move toward the joy you seek. In this case, you might move toward seeking and requesting mutual intimacy, and move away from people-pleasing and the tyranny of "should." You miss out on something: the relative ease of going along with something and not speaking up. And gain something in its place: comfort with expressing what you need and building the intimacy that you want.

You give up the things that don't truly serve your success and well-being. You make the sometimes incredibly hard decisions to leave them behind. But they don't leave an empty space—life moves too fast for that. The things you give up are replaced right away by the things you're moving toward, the things you've chosen.

You are experiencing the joy of missing out.

Courage to Share Your Joys

The scary thing about admitting what you love, what brings you joy and delight, is that it puts you out there. When you admit your joys out loud, you're showing your hand. Brené Brown says: "To let ourselves sink into the joyful moments of our lives even though we know that they are fleeting, even though the world tells us not to be too happy lest we invite disaster—that's an intense form of vulnerability."[12]

There's a fear in our admission. Our joys might be taken away. But let's stop and think closely about that fear for a moment.

If I tell you I love:

- *Ben and Jerry's* mint chocolate cookie ice cream, will you try take it away from me? Unlikely. When you hear my woeful story about how it's not available anymore in Canada, you might even want to help me get me some. Interesting.

- *Bowen Island*, a tiny enclave a stone's throw from Vancouver, Canada, my favourite place on earth, you may want to give it a google. Do it.

- *Rowing*, pushing my body and mind to the brink as I skim across open water watching the sun rise, you may be inspired to find a learn-to-row program in your community. Oh, how I hope you find one.

You may be holding your joy cards close to your chest because you're afraid someone will take them from you. Let's investigate that fear further. I've now told you some of my joys. Will you take them from me? Of course not. First of all, it's impossible. Second, if you're honest with yourself, witnessing someone else's joy gives you quiet permission to pursue your own.

Pursuing your passions gives others the courage to prioritize their own.

Remember Bubble Man?

As Nebraskan parish pastor Chad Anderson beautifully writes, "Like a contagious laugh, joy spreads wings and takes flight, hefting the burden of weighty happiness upon many shoulders."

Get at those joys. Find out who you are and where you want to go.

And go there.

Be Human

*Humans have better things to do
than pretend to be machines.*
—Amber Case

Ever feel like social media is trying to put you in a box? Craft your message in 280 characters. Explain your life story in a three-sentence bio. Put your life in a square grid.

> *You are not one thing*
> *You are not one thing*
> *You are not one thing*
> *You are not one thing*

Don't feel like you have to explain or show it all. It's not possible.
   You're too big.
   When I typed #limitless into Instagram this morning, it kicked back a whopping 2,372,595 posts. *Limitless* slogans are everywhere. Every day, advertisers, influencers, and your own insecurities tell you how and why you should overcome your limits—but what if you were to lay claim to your limits? What would that look like? For you to be thankful for them, kind to them, to even welcome them as friends?
   Well-being is having a positive relationship with our abilities *and* our limits—whatever they are. Why? Because our needs

bring us closer to one another and warm relationships are the source of our well-being. Where ability ends, relationship can begin, if we're brave enough to ask for help. That's the start of a great adventure.

Burdens

What is a burden?

The burden of a ship is its capacity for carrying cargo; its tonnage. Etymologically, "burden" is derived from the Old English *byrthen*, of West Germanic origin; related to "bear," as in a load, typically a heavy one. More often today, we think of the meaning "to cause (someone) hardship or distress." For example, a duty or responsibility, such as being forced to bear the burden of caring for your aging parents. Just look at the use of those words: "forced to bear" rather than "your capacity to carry."

When did we start demeaning the burdens of ourselves, of each other?

An archaic use of the word is a lower part in a song, a bass or accompanying part: "I would sing my song without a burden; thou bringest me out of tune" (Shakespeare).

I think the full definition is instructive:

> burden
> bur·den | \ ˈbər-dᵊn \
>
> 1: something carried
> 2: something that is hard to take—a heavy burden of sorrow
> 3: the capacity of a ship for carrying cargo
> 4: to have a heavy load or put a heavy load on
> 5: to cause to have to deal with

A burden is the capacity to carry, to hold, to serve its purpose. Do you see where I'm going here?

It has me wondering: What is my burden? What is yours?

Good Burdens

The concept of *good burdens* originates with technology philosopher Dr. Albert Borgmann, German-born professor emeritus at the University of Montana.

I am proud to call eighty-three-year-old Albert a mentor and friend. He's lived through more technological shifts than you can shake a selfie stick at. For context, when he was a teenager in Freiburg, Germany, his parents had a phone, which was very unusual for the time, and their sole source of international news was BBC Radio. When he left for America in 1958, he and his mother wrote each other almost every day. His roommates would say, "Oh my God, all these letters from your home."

The sheer quantity shocked them. Could they even begin to imagine the amount of content we are expected to manage these days? Today, the problem would not be that there are no records but that there would be no end to them. A single letter a day sounds like a holiday, doesn't it? When Albert tells me this story, he illustrates his point by telling me his oldest granddaughter recently got married but they still don't have the photos. There are too many pictures for the photographer to process. Different place and time, different problems to bear.

Today, "burden" almost sounds like a dirty word. In so many ways we've been told that if something is difficult, it's bad, and should even be avoided. Albert flips that thinking on its head. "The strange thing today is that we have hyper-information and it's not helpful because there is no value filter. It's no longer the case that we know what is to be treasured," he says. "Social media and the internet generally just overwhelm us with information. I think the result has been not a deeper understanding of reality, but a rain of bits of information. This sort of cloud of confetti obscures our vision of the world."

One of the problems of bearing the weight of contextless content confetti is that we aren't looking at our lives in terms of story. Instead of viewing our lives within the context of history, explains Albert, we're constantly focused in on a singular moment.

What is the consequence of this? How can we put our lives back in context? Albert reflects:

> The world "pre-internet" seemed to be more articulate and more eloquent. And so I think the task today is to try to recover that articulation of reality and its eloquence. It will be a difficult lesson to learn because information is like junk food. It's everywhere. It's so tempting. We're getting so used to it..... [The mind] gets distracted. There's an inability to focus. I have witnessed this shift with my students. They're not even embarrassed by not having an answer to a question. Today they think, Oh, why should I know this? Just google it.

Albert has his own strategy for helping his students build cognitive capacity: "I don't let them use computers in class. I make them take handwritten notes, which research shows are more memorable and more intelligent than when you become sort of a stenographer of what you hear."

I tell Albert about my daughter's experience, when her grade 4 teacher "taught" them about light by having them read facts on one computer window and then type notes in another. As one might imagine, my daughter was copying verbatim what she read. Light is a pretty complex concept to understand. At home, I asked her: can you tell me one thing you learned about light? She struggled for a couple of minutes and, in the end, couldn't tell me a single fact she'd internalized. I wondered aloud to Albert how physically engaging with the concept, for example seeing light refracted through a prism and writing her learning down on paper in her own words, would have deepened her understanding.

"Exactly right," replies Albert.

Learning about light longhand would have been a good burden for my daughter Madeleine.

Albert uses the examples of the burden of preparing a meal and getting everyone to show up at the table, or the burden of letter writing, gathering our thoughts, setting them down in a way that will be remembered and cherished, and perhaps even passed on to our grandchildren.

The burdensome part of these activities, he says, is usually just the task of getting across what he calls *the threshold of effort*—the burdensome aspect of the burden. As soon as you have crossed the threshold, the burden disappears.

When I ask him where this concept of good burdens originated, he says that it's all a matter of how our perspective of what a burden *is* has changed in this technological world.

> From my thinking about technology, how technology has lifted one burden after another. And now it's in this bizarre phase where it's trying to find burdens, you know, like having to go across the kitchen and turn on the radio...there's Alexa, and then there's the Smart Home that has everything for you. And I thought this burden lifting is a bad thing, you know, and of course you have to distinguish between good burdens and bad burdens.

But the question is, how do we determine the difference? Albert has a theory.

I think the culture of the table is the most hopeful place to rediscover good burdens. And as it turns out, the pandemic of the early '20s has forced people to do this. And supposedly they eat better because when you cook for yourself, it's not going to be junk food that arrives on the table and you're not going to rush through the meal.

Instead, you're more likely to savour and enjoy the fruits of your effort.

It's a powerful idea to envision yourself, in your mind's eye, at the table. Who is there with you? What are you doing? What does it all mean? If you're single, are you reading a book, enjoying a meal, and being present to that experience? Are you part of a couple, sitting across from your partner, engaged in meaningful conversation? Are you gathering as a family to eat and hear about one another's highs and lows of the day?

During dinner at my family's house, we share a *rose* (a good thing), *thorn* (a challenging thing), and a *banana* (something we are looking forward to. Our precocious youngest son, Caleb, made this one up and, luckily, it stuck).

"I think the culture of the table is the most evident, hopeful, and natural way of taking on good burdens, and I think that's where we should start," says Albert.

It's a focal point. A real anchor for your day. The human need to eat, to be social, to make meaning. It's a *good burden.*

But what are *bad burdens* and should we want to be rid of them? Is there a way in which technology solves for bad burdens? "It's important to say that every burden that's lifted comes with a cost," says Albert, and it's often difficult to anticipate what that cost will be. This is why the Amish adopt new technologies so slowly, because of their insistence on understanding the long-term impacts on their communities.

An example of a bad burden, suggests Albert, is going to the town fountain to get water. Although it was a very social activity, it was the women who carried the burden of the work and there was always the question of the purity of the water. The benefit of the water utility system outweighs the charms of the fountain in the middle of town. A bad burden is one where, as in the case of the town fountain, the benefits of having the burden lifted far outweighs the benefits that are lost.

I confess to Albert that what's coming up for me around the word "burden" is that it carries a negative connotation. It sounds heavy, like something we should want to be rid of. At least, that's what I've been told all my life. He shares one more example from his own childhood that hits very close to home: "I had most of the childhood diseases, including scarlet fever and the measles. Those were memorable experiences. You know, the way you look at the world when you're feverish and the way you're being cared for by your parents."

Little did I know that only a few months after this conversation, I'd spend the better part of a winter in hospital and then home nursing our seven year old son (Banana Caleb) back to health after a shocking sledding accident. How we'd experience utter joys and plumb wells of strength we never knew we had.

I tell Albert that the more I think about it, burdens denote *effort*. There's something *effortful* about them. And that's a good thing. It's about overcoming Tim Wu's concept of "the tyranny of convenience." We do this by extending the will, choosing to value a certain kind of burden, which is actually about our capacity—the good we are capable of. These efforts of love, they are good burdens. I want to carry them.

Yes, he says: "And if you're loving, you're building relationship."

Acknowledging Your Humanness

It's spring and the earth is unfurling. The city park I'm in is awash with daffodils, their butter tops already a foot high. My kids and I watch a one-winged pelican walk these lawns and consider aloud how it lost its other. The bird attracts a crowd. We stare at its enormous beak opening and closing, opening and closing.

People press closer, closer, iPhones in hand. Watching her, I feel both a pang of grief and wonder. She is beautiful. She is a freak. She cannot fly.

We try to give her room.

I don't know about you, but sometimes I feel like that one-winged pelican. Like I've lost a limb. Still, standing in the daylight. Showing up.

In many ways, our culture has told us that to be imperfect is to be broken and in need of fixing. But we humans have better things to do than to strive for perfection: pretending to be machines. Remember *The Stepford Wives*? It's better to be disliked for who you actually are than liked for who you're pretending to be.

> Choosing to value a certain kind of burden is actually about our capacity—the good we are capable of.

We know this. But do we believe it?

The cause of much pain and sorrow in life is the refusal to recognize and carry necessary burdens—ours and others'. Bearing with one another's humanness is perhaps the most important lesson we can learn. The less you can feel and acknowledge your own humanness, the less you can "suffer with," have compassion for, others.

In a similar vein, Amanda Quraishi, Executive Director of the Institute for Digital Civic Culture, wisely reminds us that

> In a society where we are told that we deserve an easy solution to any and all discomfort we may be personally experiencing, the value of learning to lean in to discomfort, tolerate it, and sit with it while we process it cannot be overstated. This is how we grow and get better. Individually and collectively. Not by taking the easy way out, avoiding discomfort, or passing on the challenge.[13]

Can we carry the burden of reality?

If we profess to be a loving people, we must.

It is at the outer reaches of your abilities, in your most human, vulnerable moments, that you must rely on others. Only then do you have the hope of relationship. This is the mystery. In opening yourself up to the unknown, you will find what you are looking for.

In the same park with the pelican, I perch on a comfortable rock at the edge of a playground sandbox—a good sightline of my three children gallivanting across rope bridges, slides, and spinning contraptions, glancing every few minutes to ensure they're still in my peripheral. Ten minutes into a good writing flow in my journal, I hear a mother shout in Chinese: "Move the baby! He's getting sand in his face." I follow her gaze to her husband and child, a scoop of sand hanging precariously close to the toddler's delicate eyes.

I don't know Mandarin. I don't have to. She's speaking a universal language.

Our humanness is our universal language. Our abilities and limits. Our burdens. Our capacity to bear sorrow and share joys.

Let Yourself Be

Let me tell you how I began making peace with my own humanness. I realized that I am not behind. It's not that I think I've done everything perfectly—Lord knows I've messed *a lot* of things up—but I also know this is exactly where I need to be.

You may feel like you're behind the rest of the world because you haven't accomplished your to-do list or gotten to inbox zero or have your side hustle rocking like your neighbour next door. (News flash, neither does he.) But I'm going to let you in on the great secret.

You are not behind. You are becoming.

I repeat: you are not behind. You just feel behind because we live in a time where *doing* is valued over *being*; where we feel like we must continue to be productive even during our leisure time: consuming media we've accumulated (articles, blog posts, magazines) or knocking items off our to-do lists (while we catch up on our podcast queue). When we do get some spare time, we can feel frozen because we don't know what to do with it. Could it simply be enjoyed?

I recently opened up Douglas Coupland's coffee table book *everywhere is anywhere is anything is everything*. I opened it because I couldn't read deeply; my mind was too tired (maybe you can relate to this). Instead, I turned brightly coloured pages, taking in Coupland's print-based exhibition, *Slogans for the 21st Century*. These text-based works consist of thought-provoking statements, conceived by the artist, that have been boldly printed and arranged in a manner meant to bombard the viewer, in much the same way digital memes and other advertising media do.

You are not behind.

You are becoming.

Instead of feeling bombarded, though, my eyes slowly moved from one rectangle to the next, focusing on reading each of Coupland's "slogans," until one made me stop.

It said: "When life becomes a line-up of tasks your sense of time begins to shrink."

Unstructured time is a rare commodity. So rare, in fact, that your mind may have done a double-take reading that last sentence.

Unstructured time.

As in, no structure. Space for your mind to rest and wander. Accomplishing nothing. *Nothing.*

We all exist in a highly structured time that glorifies the left brain but deprecates the right. When we rest the left brain (the language, logic, facts, detail, analysis, objectivity, linear thinking side), we stimulate the right brain (the intuition, imagination, relationships, feelings side). I know when I give myself permission to rest, completely stopping all activity to observe, sometimes wander, and enjoy the world around me, a deeper-thinking part of me emerges.

Chronic doers: We are humans and need to rest the processing capacity of our brains. We need to stop treating ourselves like machines that will never run out of batteries. We need to recognize when we need to recharge, and how.

Say it with me: *I am human. I am here. I am free to just be. It is good.*

Deep breath. Onwards.

Let us be the ones who embrace our humanity;
who would rather feel pain than feel nothing.

Quests

1. Create a blank hole in your schedule for one hour each week. Give your brain a mini-vacation. No cheating: no input or output of any kind, no screens, no laundry, no planning, no guilt. Just permission. Fill it with unhurried pleasure and space—whatever that means to you. *I'll do the same.*

2. Add 10 more items to your list of 100 Joys on page 166.

3. Reclaim the culture of the table in your own unique way.

The goal is aliveness.
The purpose is love.

Take up the good burden of being human.

Be You

It is better to be hated for what you are than to be loved for what you are not.
—André Gide

Buntzon Lake, British Columbia, a forty-five-minute drive up the mountain from the nearest town of Port Moody. It's the annual church picnic. *Dairyland vanilla ice cream cups with wooden paddle spoons. Soapy makeshift Slip 'N Slides. Barbecues chock full of burgers and wieners. Ketchup faces. Sandy feet and damp bathing suit bodies.*

The day is growing late. Adults collapsed on their floral beach chairs. Children running in packs. Life at its grandest. A sweet interlude for hurried parents and children destined for the Monday morning rush.

It's Sunday. I can smell the air: smoky, with a cold, clean cut off the lake's deep waters.

I'm barefoot. Kristen, my two-years-younger stepsister, is in overworn, spongy flip-flops. My hand-me-downs, probably. Buckets have been filled and dumped. Swims swum. We've eaten our fill. Friends have packed up into station wagons for the long drive home. Still, our parents are lingering. My sister and I are eying our next adventure when we spot a small circular sandbox on the beach. How have we not seen this before? I spot it first and plunge right in with six-year-old bravado, little-sister shadow only a step behind.

As our hands dig into the silty treasure, the pads of our feet, the paper-thin skin separating our toes, those tiny pieces of flesh register the burn.

There are signs everywhere reminding lakeside visitors to pour water over their coals before departing for the city. Our small bodies found the sole lit pit of the day.

The screams.

I do not remember screaming. Though as I write this, my body registers the panic.

It's unclear who finds us, but found we are and, by some genius, tossed into the frigid lake water. Our screams eventually dampen to a whimper. I recall the stillness of the lake, the calm of dusk as we sat legs-deep on fold-up chairs licking Popsicles while Dad and my stepmom, Grace, cobbled together a plan. The seven of us kids were probably there. I only remember Kristen and me. Maybe I don't remember Kristen. Maybe, because I've been told the story so many times, I've written her in.

I later remember her at the hospital where we sat soaking our feet in bedpans, playing with plastic syringes, sucking up the water and aiming it back between our toes.

This is my very first memory.

It wasn't until I wrote and shared it at a narrative writing group that I began seeing this core memory in a brand new way. For most of my life, I read this early impression—a young girl literally burned, singed, scarred—as a sign of a deeply painful childhood. When I gathered the courage to read it aloud to the members of our small circle, they heard a very different story. Like the dusk-lit lake, they reflected back to me: care, concern, compassion. I left flooded with gratitude.

Seeing the way in which a memory I had always considered painful could be reconsidered from a different perspective, it made me wonder at all of my memories. Could they all be reconsidered in a new way? What did this say about my story? Who was I, really?

The same thing can happen when we reconsider the word "burden." Now that we know burden can also mean *capacity*, let's explore it as a place of potential, of possibility. Let's explore the capacity to be you. Fully you. Not shadow you. Not the used-to-be you. Not the you you *should* be.

You. Precious and peculiar, brilliant and bruised you.

Avoid Avoidance

It's never been easier to hide from the truth of your experience. The internet is the perfect place to escape from life's too-muchness.

Someone doesn't like you. *Ouch*. Instagram.

Someone offends you. *Ouch*. Facebook.

Someone getting ahead of you. *Ouch*. TikTok.

Something getting under your skin. *Yuck*. Netflix.

Anywhere but here, being you, right?

"Technology can be used as a way to avoid direct encounter, as a shield," writes David Abram in *Becoming Animal*, "to ward off whatever frightens, as a synthetic heaven or haven in which to hide out from the distressing ambiguity of the real." I know I have used technology in this way. Have you?

The Discipline of Gratitude

I have found one person who had the courage to embrace his me-ness, his too-much and not-enoughness. His name was Henri Nouwen.

What's your first memory? What does it say about you? Is there a new way of seeing it? Who will you trust with your story?

People have called him many things: a priest, an author, a spiritual guide, a natural mystic. His books have sold millions of copies and continue to resonate deeply with people from all walks of life. In 2000, when asked to share the book that had most influenced her life, Hillary Clinton chose Nouwen's *The Return of the Prodigal Son*. The following sentence in particular, she said in an interview with Oprah Winfrey, hit her "like a lightning bolt"[14]:

> The discipline of gratitude is the explicit effort to acknowledge that all I am and have is given to me as a gift of love, a gift to be celebrated with joy.

"I had never thought of gratitude as a habit or discipline before," she explained, "and I discovered that it was immensely helpful to do so."

I first discover Henri when I'm eighteen years old and gifted with a 365-day flip calendar of his quotes and reflections.

"All I want to say to you is 'You are the Beloved,' and all I hope is that you can hear these words spoken to you with all the tenderness and force that love can hold. My only desire is to make these words reverberate in every corner of your being."[15]

The longer I journey with Henri, the better I understand his near-universal appeal. He sought a kind of language of the heart that each generation has to create anew. He was also a wounded healer who, in so many words and ways, presented an inviting vision of life—one grounded in place, with a people, fully present, and alive to wonder.

It's all I want. Maybe it's all any of us wants.

In the breathless race of the digital era, many of us feel driven by restlessness, overwhelm, and fear of never-enoughness. Though his writing, speaking, and mentorship, Henri had an uncanny ability to shed light on our false selves—the parts of us seeking power, success, and approval at all costs—and in the process, revealing the true desires of our hearts: to be disarmed, to be known, and to come close enough to love to let it touch us.

"Can we carry the burden of reality? How can we remain open

to all human tragedies and aware of the vast ocean of human suffering...It is only through facing up to the reality of our world that we can grow into our own responsibility,"[16] he wrote.

After a string of prominent teaching positions at Yale, Notre Dame, and Harvard, Henri abandoned the academic hallways of power to live out the remainder of his days as Henri "Just Me" Nouwen in an obscure community in North Toronto. This morning, nearly twenty years after receiving that calendar, I find myself at L'arche Daybreak: staying in Henri's old home, where he lived with and worked as an assistant to mentally disabled men during the final ten years of his life. Here, he wrote some of his most important books. A print of Rembrandt's *The Return of the Prodigal Son*, a painting Henri spent years interpreting, hangs above the fireplace, silently anchoring the common room.

Inside this simple retreat house, sunlight is silently dancing through the window dressings. I'm pulling dusty copies of Flannery O'Connor and Evelyn Underhill down from the shelves. I feel like I'm standing in the middle of a story. I've just begun my sojourn, and already I feel I'm walking on water. I've committed to a year-long journey of reading, and in some cases, rereading, Nouwen's nearly forty books on the spiritual life.

Henri's profound capacity for friendship, childlike love of celebration (Henri was a party animal and had a particular love of the circus), and ability to accept the things he cannot change, draw me in. He's helping me discover the woman I want to be. Perhaps more than anything, my year-long journey with Henri has revealed the slow power of presence in our productivity-obsessed age.

Holy Inefficiency

Henri's entire life, in fact, displayed a holy inefficiency[17]—a total commitment to the slow work of love.

When an intense young man reached out to a small group of prominent spiritual writers by letter, Henri invited this stranger to live with him for a month so he could mentor him in person.

Most writers jealously protect their schedules and privacy, but

Henri was always closing the gap between himself and others. It is this kind of radical openness and brave intimacy that I believe our hearts are desperately searching for.

A total commitment to the slow work of love.

Perhaps what I most need is what you also need: to confront your fears, let go of false securities, and enter the stillness where hope and joy can be found.

Henri articulates something I know but still need to hear.

I want to be free of the pressures to be relevant, spectacular, and powerful.

I want to know I am accepted just as I am.

I want an experience of the eternal, not an argument.

I want to know what's true about love.

I pray, dear reader, these are the things you need on the journey. Together, let's risk being known and loving bravely.

You deserve a space to be you.

The Ship That Is You

A burden is the capacity of a ship, so let's look closely at the ship that is you.

Have you ever been aboard a ferry, a modern cruise liner, somehow simultaneously sleek and elegant while being impossibly huge? Or a beautiful old three-masted frigate with polished wood and flapping sails?

I want you to think of your life as a ship.

Setting Course

A ship is not built to sit pretty and clean, untarnished, by the shore. It might begin that way, but a ship forever moored is a heartbreak. It may be safe in harbour, but that's not what it's built for; it's intended to venture into open waters, cross vast oceans, and land triumphant in new ports, over and over. On the way, it will encounter storms and must weather them.

The ship metaphor is near and dear to me. It's been significant since my early adult life when a woman in my church, a young mother, printed off a picture of a ferry and covered it with hand-written notes, reminding me of my capacity and purpose. Then, years later, I made an amazing discovery as I began researching what goes into building and maintaining a ship: each stage could be mapped perfectly onto our own.

Ships take years to be built properly. Only experienced captains are at the helm, no wannabes allowed. Nothing, from conception to completion to use and maintenance, is left to chance. And they get christened with the best champagne!

There are a number of distinct phases of a ship's existence. So, if you don't feel ready yet to unfurl your sails and set out in open waters, you're not alone.

Design

First, the ship is designed. To draw up blueprints, you need to know where the ship is going. What kind of water is it passing through? How many people aboard? What is the ship's purpose? That will help you know what kind of ship to build.

For we "human ships," our design is our DNA, and whatever more we believe goes into the making of our lives before we start living them. We enter the world with the blueprint of human evolution: we are intelligent, social mammals evolved to live in communities of extended families, create tools to solve our problems, be aware of our own mortality, use language, experience a wide range of emotions, and survive and flourish by altering the environment around us to suit the needs of our relatively fragile bodies.

We have no control over this part of our existence. We are born as we are. But there's tremendous value in reviewing this stage, in going over our blueprints. We are all built in different ways, with various strengths and challenges.

What kind of ship are you? Do you have a deep, streamlined hull for solitary exploration of dark, open waters? Are you a sturdy, reliable ferry delighting in serving others and smoothing the way? Are you a quick, streamlined cutter zipping with rootless joy from place to place? When you understand what kind of ship you are, you're far closer to understanding your mission and purpose.

We are a varied and beautiful regatta with no bad designs. We are all seaworthy.

Build

The next step of the life of a ship is the building stage. This can take years. It's unforgiving work. It takes a lot of people to make this happen.

The art and industry of building ships has always been hard—it was hard for ancient peoples, and it's still hard today. It's beautiful, terrible work. Crafting and constructing something that will not only endure the immensely powerful sea but float and travel upon it remains a task calling for skilled and hard labour. Modern ships are no easier—people are still injured and even die in the effort. It takes years to build a ship of any substantial size.

If you're an adult, the building of your ship is probably complete: the toil and sacrifice of your parents and caregivers supporting, nurturing, and raising you before sending you out into open waters. The effort of your teachers and people in your community to prepare you with the knowledge, skills, and values they believed would best prepare you for the deep blue sea of your life.

How do you feel about your shipbuilders? Did they do a good job? Maybe, for you, this question brings feelings of regret, sadness, or even anger. Like everyone, the people who built you are imperfect humans. The story of your construction includes good and bad intentions, triumphs and tragedies, skillful jobs and terrible mistakes. The building of a ship, metaphorical or not, remains an intensely human undertaking. No ship or human on earth is made ready for life without the touch of human hands.

As before, there's value in reflecting on this step, even if it's too late to have a hand in it. How were you built? What was your "shipyard" like? Were your builders experts, or amateurs? Were they passionate, or indifferent? The value in this reflection is understanding how your construction has shaped the way you sail. There's an old saying that there's blood in the hull of every ship, that the pain and sacrifice inevitable in any large, important undertaking end up baked into the final product. As you think about the process of building the person you are, the person sitting here now, what events do you think altered the final product? What are the elements of your development that you want to compensate and correct for, and what are the things you love and want to lean into?

One last thing. However imperfect the people who raised the ship that is you might have been, I encourage you to extend gratitude to everyone who did their best. No matter how unhappy our history may be, it is good that we are all here, and we all have a path ahead of us. You are worthy of being here. Be grateful for it.

Outfitting

Third, the ship is outfitted. In the Age of Sail, this meant gleaming brass railings, tethers, and cleats, even stained glass windows in cabins. Beautiful figureheads would arch proudly across the prow, leading the way into the unknown. The French SS *Normandie*, the largest luxury liner of her day when launched in 1932, was named "the Ship of Light," as every inch of her interior was filled with chandeliers, hand-painted murals, and polished wood.

> What kind of ship are you? What makes up your blueprint?

Outfitting a ship is the stage that reflects its character. It's when the distinctive personality of the vessel shines through.

What about you? What's your style? Where do your joys lie? Do you like things no-nonsense and minimal, or do you love surrounding yourself with beauty? Are you happiest in the limelight, or in quietly getting the job done? Your outfitting includes the skills and abilities you've developed along the way.

What uniquely makes you?

Launch

For some of us, this is a stage of our voyages in recent memory, maybe even still forthcoming. For others, it may be a moment in our past that we look back on with fondness. Maybe when you moved out of the house. Maybe when you finished college or began your first job.

Throughout history, launching a ship, however humble, is a special occasion and nearly always accompanied with fanfare. Every culture has evolved sincere, joyful rituals around this moment—releasing birds, opening champagne, making noise—reminiscent of our sweet sixteens, our christenings or confirmations, our bar and bat mitzvahs, and so on. The moment when a labour of love breaks out into the world is a moment that every community in human history has known is call for celebration and joy.

Our first, or "maiden," voyage is not only momentous but uniquely intense. We are out in open waters. We are making our own moves, for the first time. We are trying ourselves out, testing our speed and limitations. We will make mistakes; we don't know all of our capabilities, and we've never exercised them before. But these steps and these mistakes are immensely valuable; through them, we are bravely learning to be our best selves, something we absolutely cannot learn if we remain fearfully anchored in port.

How was your launch celebrated? Was there fanfare, or was it a quiet affair? Did you feel ready for your maiden voyage? What was it—college, a career, the military, marriage? How well did those maiden voyages go? What did you learn from them?

The best thing about our maiden voyages is that as long as we're alive, we can go on another one. Whether our first voyage was regal or awkward, perfectly executed or a trial of errors, it won't be our last.

If we remain at sea, there will always be another journey.

You are the ship.

Consider all the things you are in one day:

- A sleeper
- A journaller
- A breakfast maker
- A walker
- A teacher
- An arguer
- A lover
- A worker
- A coffee maker
- A coffee drinker
- A cleaner
- A conversationalist

What event in your life do you consider your maiden voyage? How well did it go, and what did you learn?

- A leader
- A fashionista
- A reader
- A joke maker
- A Twitter-er
- A gardener
- A procrastinator
- An artist
- A dancer
- A friend
- A spouse
- A texter
- An errand runner
- A biker
- A cook
- A dishwasher
- A ukulele player
- A neighbour
- A TV watcher
- A snuggler

Try fitting all of that in your Twitter bio. Attempting to fit yourself onto the internet is like trying to shove your entire body into an infant's sock. *Impossible. Laughable. Exhausting. Futile.* Be suspicious of any place, and anyone, where you must reduce yourself to fit.

What have you been hiding? Don't settle for small. Stretch out and find your big.

Set sail.

Let us be the ones who love ourselves;
who embrace our strengths and weaknesses alike.

Quests

1. Find a favourite photo of yourself where you look most you—*most alive*. Spend a few minutes noticing where you are, what you're wearing, who you're with, and what you're doing. Bring an element of that *you* into your life today.

2. Find a photo of yourself as a kid. Reconnect to the joys there. Prying open chestnuts under a canopy of leaves. Swinging straight up to the sky. Filling notebooks with sketches, poems, and plans. What do you love about that little you?

3. Add 10 more lines to your list of 100 Joys.

The goal is aliveness.
The purpose is love.

Take up the good burden of being you.

III

BEING LED BY JOY

A ship in harbor is safe
but that is not what ships are built for.
—John A. Shedd

In her book *The Happiness Project*, Gretchen Rubin made an important discovery. She realized that her efforts to lighten up in her parenting, prioritizing more time for projects and presence with her daughters, had enormous payoff.

Studies show marital satisfaction typically nosedives after the first child is born and picks up again once children leave home. "Nevertheless, despite these findings," she writes, "I had to reject the expert's argument that children don't bring happiness. Because they do. Not always in a moment-to-moment way, perhaps, but in a more profound way."

She calls this kind of happiness, *fog happiness*. It's all around you, transforming the atmosphere, yet ephemeral, elusive. When you try to examine it, it vanishes.

"Fog happiness is the kind of happiness you get from activities that, closely examined, don't really seem to bring much happiness at all—yet somehow they do."

Gretchen, I've got an answer for you. They're called good burdens.

This is a good place to revisit Albert Borgmann's original articulation, I think.

> Consider…the burden of preparing a meal and getting everyone to show up at the table and sit down. Or the burden of reading poetry to one another or going for a walk after dinner. Or the burden of letter-writing—gathering our thoughts, setting them down in a way that will be remembered and cherished and perhaps passed on to our grandchildren. The burdensome part of these activities is actually just the task of getting across a threshold of effort. As soon as you have crossed the threshold, the burden disappears.

Like Gretchen describes, many activities that bring me joy are not all that enjoyable while they're happening. Writing a book. Parenting my children. Getting out for exercise. Gathering up my thoughts in a letter for a faraway friend. I keep going with these activities because I've been around long enough to know the long-term gains.

It may be a little masochistic to think of finishing writing a book as birthing a baby, but it's the best analogy I can think of. Would I prolong labour for even a minute? Hell, no. So it is with writing. Steady on to the finish but not a moment more. There is joy on the other side.

This may explain why people who are happy with technology, occupying digital spaces where we now spend the lion's share of our waking hours, are using it differently.

People Who Are Happy with Technology Do Things Differently

You've probably spent time on your smartphone, laptop, or tablet today. You've almost certainly had a Zoom chat this week. If you've got kids, they're likely spending more time than ever on social media, playing video games, or sharing memes with their friends.

None of this technology is going to go away. Very, very few of us will be able to move to an Old Order Amish community, or go off the grid and escape most modern technology. However we may want to believe it, realistically, we do not have the unfettered choice to live without technology.

There's good news, though. Research shows that people who are happy with technology do things in three particular ways. Emotional ethnographer Pamela Pavliscak made this discovery after having hundreds of people track their highs and lows with technology in diaries.

I have spent half a decade encouraging people *to disconnect from the internet*, so you can imagine this was a tough pill to swallow. In addition to discovering Dr. Pavliscak's work, I gradually developed a personal realization as I interviewed mindful tech leaders and creators—the wisest, most joyful people I could find—on the *JOMO(cast)* about the nitty gritty, the real tech tools and online habits they had mastered to accomplish their dreams without getting distracted or drained.

"If you ask people whether technology makes them happy, they will look puzzled," says Pamela. "Most will talk instead about how technology is taking up too much time, distracting them from real life, and generally making them miserable. But what about the positives?"

She says the difference is part mindset, part action. So, what do people who are happy with technology do? I wanted to find out.

How Happy People Use the Internet

It turns out that the people flourishing with technology use it in very intentional ways. First off, they use it to serve larger goals. *They have a destination.* They also have a deep sense of their values. They're protected from getting pulled off course by social contagion or FOMO, wanting what other people have.

> People who are happiest with technology use it to love, to carry good burdens.

In her study, Pamela Pavliscak discovered these individuals use technology for three primary purposes: Caring, Creativity, and Community, deepening warm relationships in the process. You might say people who are happiest with technology use it to *love*, to *carry good burdens*.

Often when we think about our relationship with technology, we think, Oh, it's distracting. It's pulling me away from real life. And so we frame a lot of our well-being [as though] we need to have this time offline to kind of rebalance things. There's a little bit of truth in that, of course. But what I found when digging into people's daily records of what was making them feel unhappy, it was about this distortion. And two major things stood out to me.

The first distortion Pamela found was that of *time*. People feeling like they are losing time, that it's going too fast, creating a false sense of urgency.

When we're thinking about technology as designers, [we] are often tasked with making something seamless, efficient, easy, taking away all the friction points. That might lead to our time distortion idea right there, where it's really easy to move through and get lost in it. But it also takes away the emotional register that we might have as well.

So, the second distortion is emotional.

Attention-seeking technology gets that attention by maximizing our emotions in a weird way. What makes content 'go viral' is intense emotion, intense anger and outrage, [which is] intense fear. Those are the emotions that are fuelling our attention, and it's unnatural for us to be in that kind of heightened state all of the time.

When we're constantly in that state, it feels like we're not ourselves and *our reality is not the same*. Those two aspects, time and emotional distortion, really stood out to me...It's fostering a sense of self that doesn't quite ring true.

In other words, *you don't know who or where you are or where you are going.*

Setting Course

Pamela suggests that in those moments when tech feels bad, you should ask: Is this experience distorting my relationship, emotional life, or sense of time? If it is, take that as a cue to step back and reflect.

"When you do step back, it is about grounding in real time and space to realign with what you value and how you want to be spending your time. When you step back, ask yourself what you are actually trying to do."

What do I care about? Why am I here? It's attentive and effortful work.

"The renewal of societies and organizations can go forward only if someone cares," wrote social scientist John Gardner.[18] People who are happy with technology are also led by joy; they use it to do things they care about. They have a certain give-a-shit-ness to them. When you care, you want to do something *useful*. When you care, you're willing to *commit*.

Be Useful

Do external things distract you?
Then make time for yourself to learn something worthwhile;
stop letting yourself be pulled in all directions.
—Marcus Aurelius, *Meditations*

I *need something to do 'cause I can't watch the news. No, I* *can't watch the news anymore.* So sing the cast of *Come from Away*, the Broadway musical about 9/11, as they watch the terror unfolding on their screens.

I need something to do.

As we discussed earlier, in the Discovering Your Joys section, we need something to do. This helps explain why so much of the world took up bread baking during the COVID-19 pandemic. We were seeking out creative ways to make meaning in the midst of global upheaval.

We learned to play instruments. Zoomed loved ones. Checked on neighbours. Volunteered. Planted gardens. Wrote letters.

We began noticing and nurturing the relationships and activities that bring meaning and joy. We sought out opportunities to be useful.

How a Burden Becomes a Joy

A burden can become a joy. How? By loving in service of the common good—creating, caring, and building community wherever you are.

Small, Sane Actions

Lindsay Coulter, an environmentalist and public engagement officer with the David Suzuki Foundation for more than thirteen years, believes that small, sane actions are the key to staying anchored in this world and making a positive contribution.

What first drew me to Lindsay is how her environmental education work seeks to help others become whole people who think about the way they're impacting not only the environment but one another, the entire ecosystems in which they live. It's a vital mission.

What began for Lindsay as daily environmental action tips (*Top 5 things you can do to have a green vacation; My favourite green cleaning recipes*) evolved to focus more on people's relationships to each other *and* the planet.

"They need to know where to find a rain barrel in Winnipeg and how to avoid plastic produce bags at the grocery store. But people are also looking for places to have conversations and show up," says Lindsay. "Like having the courage to have a conversation about 'What if none of this matters?' or 'How do I start a conversation with my family or neighbour about my vow not to fly this year?'"

The usefulness of her work extends beyond the practical to the deeper place of *relationship*, and she believes this can happen online. In every creative contribution, she's asking: how do our relationships matter in the scope of our environmental footprint?

Stay Attached to This World

There's a lot of things that I'm very proud of and lots of things that really still bother me," says Lindsay, who lives in Victoria,

British Columbia, where she also helps lead her children's outdoor school. "I think so much of what I seek to do is try to pull back the layers. I'm not particularly good at it myself in terms of revealing vulnerabilities and challenges online. But I feel like the more our online and offline spaces reflect one another, then the better off we'll all be."

It's why she is so passionate about gathering people in the real world. Ultimately, the goal is to help others pull back the layers to see their own capacities. For example, the capacity to sit in a circle, to watch people's body language and experience all of the emotions that come with it—the discomfort and the joys. She says,

> That's why it's so important to keep coming back to nature. We're so restless, distracted, and going numb. We've collectively and individually done a lot of damage because we're not being present. When you're numb, you're disconnected from yourself and other people in the world around you. I stay the course because I believe that humans have the capacity be creative and kind and generous. It is good to be an active participant in this human experience.

Lindsay is not afraid of the messy work of restoration. In his meditations, Marcus Aurelius wrote resolutely,

> Don't waste the rest of your time here worrying about other people—unless it affects the common good. It will keep you from doing anything *useful*. You'll be too pre-occupied with what so-and-so is doing, and why, and what they're saying, and what they're thinking, and what they're up to, and all the other things that throw you off and keep you from focusing on your own mind.
>
> Avoid every random and irrelevant thing.

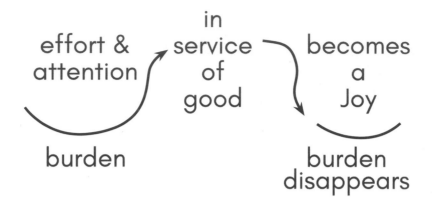

effort & attention — in service of good — becomes a Joy

burden → burden disappears

"Joy is the other side of burden"

It can look like the internet is little more than an ocean of *random and irrelevant things*. But if you come back to Pamela Pavliscak's discoveries, you have an anchor point. You can happily make use of technology to creatively contribute.

In his book *The Practice*, Seth Godin helped me to see that "When you choose to produce creative work, you're solving a problem. Not just for you, but for those who are lucky enough to experience your contribution."

Creativity is about serving others with your gifts. Be useful: offer something substantial and real. Recognize the generosity of creating.

What will your contribution be?

Your Environment Supports Your Capacity to Serve

Your physical and digital environments affect your capacity to creatively contribute.

For example, if all the characters in *Come from Away*, each based on real women and men of Gander, Newfoundland, sat staring at their Twitter feeds instead of picking up the phones and asking *What can we do?* on September 11, we'd have no story. Certainly no Tony Award–winning musical. Instead, the tiny island community housed, fed, and clothed nearly seven thousand passengers and crew for multiple days when thirty-eight airliners were forced to land at Gander International Airport on September 11, 2001.

When there wasn't room, they turned off their TVs and made some.

What can we do?

Your physical and digital environments have the capacity to increase or decrease your capacity to be useful. The first step is to eliminate distraction.

Eliminate Distraction

The biggest perpetrator of distraction is your smartphone. It's an amazing little thing, isn't it? An alarm clock, a newspaper, a library of books, a video and music player, a computer. It's even a telephone!

The utility of the smartphone is rooted in a tech design concept known as convergence: creating multipurpose devices that absorb the function of as many other devices as possible. By itself, the concept of convergence isn't bad; it leads to devices that are more convenient, portable, and affordable, since you're buying one thing instead of many. But the dark side of convergence, especially when it comes to smartphones, lies in the attention economy.

When you use your smartphone for your alarm clock, you're putting Facebook, newsfeeds, games, and messenger apps right in your path. The proximity and convenience of all the functions of this one device means that when you pick up your phone to do something—or even just have it nearby acting as an alarm clock, stereo, or TV—you're extremely likely to do one of those *other* things, and about as likely to completely *forget* what you originally picked your phone up for in the first place.

For example, I recently began learning the ukulele. I learned by videos taped by a local teacher and watched them on our iPad. I was encouraged to use a tuning app on my phone called GuitarTuna (cute, right?). All of this tech had the opportunity to pull me into other activities. The way I counteracted these distractions was to make is social. I sat on my living-room floor with my family all around, which kept me focused on the task of learning, not bopping down the email app. I also keep my devices free of unnecessary apps and organized in folders. Both of these digital and physical environmental choices kept me doing what I wanted to do: pluck the little green instrument.

The solution to getting hijacked by the other features on your phone is to *consciously reject convergence* when it comes to your smartphone. Do all the features of your smartphone qualify as being needed in your space? Almost certainly not, so don't let them be.

Go Analog

Need to know what time it is? There are wonderful things called watches and clocks. Get one in a style that brings you joy. Want to take a short, controlled break to read the news? Keep a real newspaper or magazine in your space: it only does one thing, lets you read the news, and it has a bounded beginning and end; there is a limit as to how much content is available.

The truth is, our smartphone usually has no place in a productive or creative space: the vast majority of its features are nothing more than life-taking distractions from the things we really need in that moment.

Consider a beautiful, joyful, personal analog version of the things you actually *need* your phone to do, and leave your smartphone itself outside of your sacred space. It doesn't belong there.

I'm editing this page at an outdoor table using pen and paper. My phone is at home. I'm sipping my favourite beverage from a travel cup and slipping effortlessly into the work. This is all I need. What few items do you need to do your best work?

Put Joy in Your Path

The simplest and most pleasurable part of creating a life-giving environment, one in which we feel encouraged to creatively contribute, is to add in the things we *do* want.

One of the cornerstones of the 12-Step program of addiction recovery popularized by Alcoholics Anonymous is the concept that addiction is triggered by "people, places, and things," meaning you're much more likely to engage in your habitual behaviour when you're in the environment where you usually do them.

Consider the space where you spend the most time doing the things that matter to you—whether that's your work, creative activities, passion projects, playing games or reading books, spending time with family, anything that really matters.

Make it as easy to engage in these activities as possible.

I asked creative entrepreneur Jen Duffin, a Montreal-based weaver (Nova Mercury Design), how she makes creativity flourish for herself and her family. Her answer was simple: make those creative outlets present, visible, readily available, and convenient. Her weaving tools are right where she likes to sit and spend her time—her living room—and craft and art stations are scattered wherever her children go to look for things to do, not tucked away in a closet, out of sight and out of mind.

What are the things you want to do more of? What are the creative contributions you want to make? The physical trappings of those things should be front and centre, always visible: a kind of anti-friction.

Put that painting easel, sketchbook, journal, vintage typewriter, stack of books, outline, tablet, or computer where you'll always see it and be able to quickly engage with it, and surround it with the things you need to make it an inviting and joyful activity.

In short, make environmental changes, both to your physical and digital space, to make it as easy as possible to do the things you *want* to do.

Add in Nature

I am writing at a picnic table in Toronto's High Park. *Free.* Typing on a seven-year-old computer. *Not free, but functional.* Entertained by sparrows, robins, and a kaleidoscope of butterflies dancing in the twilight thrush. *Free.* While my sister-in-law helps care for our kids. *By some grace of God, free.* Behind me a steady stream of bikers, rollerbladers, and runners lap the perimeter of the park. *Free.* I notice the shape of a tiny wing imprinted in the green tabletop I'm working on. *Not free for the bug. It probably cost him his life.*

How did we forget that old cliché, *The best things in life are free?*

The last piece of optimizing your environment is to engage with the biggest and most powerful environment of all, what tech workers have sometimes called The Big Room: nature.

The positive effects of connection with nature, however big or small, are well documented for promoting physical and mental well-being, creativity, productivity, alertness, and more. Having at least some contact with nature each day is an essential element of joy. Full stop.

Make the outdoors part of your creative space at least once a week, no matter what it takes. If your creative or productive work can be done outside, and the weather allows, try it. I've written a great deal of this book sitting at that beat-up picnic table in the park and it's worked wonders for my creativity. Being out of doors is an essential reminder that I am a small part of an immense world. The stimuli—sounds, smells, and sights—never fail to help me make deeper connections, weaving seemingly divergent thoughts into a cohesive whole. In nature, it all fits together.

If you can't work outdoors, make contact with nature a short daily ritual: begin or end your day with a walk, or do it as part of a midday break. If possible, arrange or change your creative space to allow nature in: have windows that let you see the natural world; add living things like plants, flowers, or small pets into your space.

Your environment, the water you're surrounded by and immersed in every day, is one of the most powerful influences on your ability to thrive in every domain of your life—physically, mentally, and spiritually. Scientific evidence suggests that exposure to nature activates specific reward circuits in the brain associated with dopamine release that give us a sense of purpose, joy, and energy to pursue our goals.[19]

When you mindfully assess the contents of your environment, take control and make it a life-giving space, you set yourself up for amazing work, play, connection, and creation.

When you start working toward a long-term goal, make sure you've created an environment for that goal to be achieved—and get ready to succeed.

The Change You Wish To See

You've created some space. Now, to sustain the desire to care, create, and build community, you need a larger vision.

Can you see it? What is the change you wish to see in the world?

Here is my wish.

That we will be the ones who reach for our loved ones before we reach for our phones. We are the ones who walk our streets with ears and eyes wide open, seeking to offer a smile, create a

What are the things you want to do more of? How can you make physical space for them?

moment of conversation, see the need that needs meeting (garbage to pick up, an elderly person struggling to open a door, a lonely neighbour sitting on their front stoop). My wish is that you and I will be the weavers, joyfully missing out on the right things to take up good burdens. With each act of communion, we are weaving a community.

One more thing: don't underestimate the generosity and simple power of asking *How can I help?* "Nothing," wrote Tolstoy, "can make our life, or the lives of other people, more beautiful than perpetual kindness."

My wish is that you and I will be the weavers, joyfully missing out on the right things to take up good burdens.

One day, my kids and I went hunting in the alley for bits of brick and rock. We came home with a windfall. I set out a basket of acrylic paint on our steaming hot table out back and we painted (and grumbled) for an hour. Before us, a mosaic of colour emerged: chipped grey edges turned to watermelons, rounded stones became rocket ships and beaches and, my favourite, triangular brick pizza slices. Once we were finished, we carried them out one by one to place in our front garden near the sidewalk edge. Ever since, we've watched wistful toddlers stop and play seek-and-find with our colourful offerings.

What can you do? How can you be useful?

Maybe all you've got are painted rocks. That's enough.

Make it about what you can give. Joy will follow.

Let us be the ones who are generous;
who give others our whole hearts and attention.

Quests

1. Begin asking today, how can I be useful?

2. Write about the world you hope to help make.

3. Ask yourself, what are some physical and digital environmental changes I can make today to support the things I want to do?

The goal is aliveness.
The purpose is love.

Take up the good burden of being useful.

Be Committed

Be impeccable with your word.
—Don Miguel Ruiz, *The Four Agreements*

One day, Twitter recommended I follow Elissa Joy Watts: a self-described "Freelance Writer and Joy Scout." *Sometimes the algorithm just knows.* Within twenty-four hours of clicking her profile, I receive a direct message.

> *Elissa: Rarely do I investigate the strangers who begin following me on social media. I, like you, prize time away from screens and as such, find myself putting down my phone as quickly as possible most days. BUT! Today my children are enjoying pancakes at my parents' home and my husband and I are enjoying a lazy morning. I noticed that a dear friend, Darian, follows you too and thought, "Do I know this person?" So off I went, chasing you around the internet. And HALLELUJAH! I am so glad I did. I will deliver a hug in person if/when we get back to Toronto. Girl, you're on the right train. JOMO! YES! I love it all. Be blessed this Saturday morning (or afternoon, as the case may be).*

Within weeks Elissa and I are swapping emails, then texting like old friends. She sends me a photo of her wedding with the challenge: "Name six people in this photo." I can, with little difficulty. It turns out we had orbited around one another back home in Vancouver but somehow never met. Her husband Steve's sister dated my brother in high school. We have numerous mutual friends. Elissa's dad worked with one of my younger brothers. We laugh at the sheer volume of serendipity surrounding our growing friendship.

Soon comes the turn in our story no one is expecting.

> *Elissa: Team Watts is coming to Toronto in the fall!!!!!!!!!!!!!! STEVE landed a post-doc at U of T after all!!!!!!!!!! Shhhhhhhhhh. Papers aren't signed but I had to share. We get to be IRL friends soon. Xx*

Elissa begins sending me all of her questions about Toronto— schools, neighbourhoods, parks, cost of living. The wheels in my head begin to turn. My husband, Michael, and I have talked about sharing our home with another family for years. It's not for everyone, but we've always felt the pull toward community living. So it wasn't a stretch for me to send this email:

> *Christina: Hey Elissa, We live in the Junction which is on the west side, north from High Park. We adore our neighbourhood—it's filled with down-to-earth creatives and is entirely walkable. That said, it's a bit of a way to the campus but we have a U of T PhD student who lives with us and he doesn't find it too bad of a commute. We are big on community living. We'd happily make room for a certain fivesome. Big hugs to you this warm and rainy Monday, Christina*

*Elissa (**seconds later**): WAIT—are you serious?! Truly—*
are you serious? Because if you are, we'd happily carry on
with that discussion. We're big on community living too
and because we'll only be living there for a year, we've
been hypothesizing about some kind of shared living expe-
rience. If you're serious about taking in a team of five, let's
jam. #tenpeopleoneshower #TeamWattstakesYYZ

For a year, we commit to sharing our home with another family of five.

Ten People, One shower

The Wattses move in. A few months into our experiment, we're still adjusting, crying, rejoicing—and, oh, did we mention their newborn baby? It feels like we are walking on water, then drowning, then pulling one another up for air.

We thought our six-year-old boys would get along famously. They didn't. We have to work at finding ways for them to connect. We thought the Wattses would have enough room. They didn't. We have to reconfigure the house all over again and give them an extra bedroom. We thought it would be challenging to distribute the household labour. It isn't. Everyone simply pitches in and the work continues to get done day after day. We weren't sure how meal-planning would go. It turns out Elissa went to culinary school and is a master strategist, so food prep and feeding the families has been streamlined and straightforward.

Little miracles happen every day. Steve and I walk the kids to school in the morning after making lunches, feeding six hungry children, and helping put on dozens of pieces of snow gear. When I circle back to the house, I come home to a spotless kitchen.

The CBC shows up to tell our story.

This is the power of teamwork. As we like to say around here, "Teamwork makes the dream work." It's not easy. Not by a long shot. Through this experience, I am beginning to understand what Henri Nouwen means when he writes "to be hospitable is to liberate fearful hearts." Yes, even our own.

When we commit, we begin to be seen. There's no hiding.

Remember the Harvard Grant Study? Psychologist George Vaillant, who directed the study for over thirty years, summed up the findings as follows: "warmth of relationships throughout life has the greatest positive impact on 'life satisfaction.'" Another of his observations is worth repeating here: "Happiness is love. Full stop."

We all share a hunger for community. A place to belong. What kind of community do you dream of? What are you willing to do to create it?

Make A Commitment to Happiness

People from Scandinavian countries like Denmark, Sweden, and Iceland are often talked about and studied as some of the happiest populations in the world. One big variable in their lifestyle is that, compared to most other western cultures, Scandinavians have a high rate of membership in social groups like charity organizations, fraternities, or clubs, and most report having at least one, if not several, standing social commitments each week, such as a regular dinner party, book club, or game night.

When we measure up these behavioural patterns against the

> **What does your ideal community look like? How will go about creating it?**

findings from people like Vaillant, it's easy to see why they're so happy: they're creating long-term commitments to participation in activities that will put them continuously in the path of creating and nurturing *warm relationships.*

Consider your current commitment patterns. Are you addicted to distraction?

I once heard a woman talk about how she used to love taking bites out of dozens of projects and pursuits. One day, her mom asked which of one of the projects she enjoyed the most. The woman stopped long enough to realize she wasn't really enjoying any of them. "I realized I'd been eating ego cake," she said. *Slice after slice after slice.* Which did she enjoy the most? None of them.

Who and what will you commit to?

The Power of Social Commitments

There is great power in social commitments. By having the social obligations that come with attending organized gatherings, more time is spoken for in structured ways that leave fewer opportunities to sit at home endlessly scrolling through social media, or being lonely.

"A commitment device is a choice that an individual makes in the present which restricts his own set of choices in the future, often as a means of controlling future impulsive behavior and limiting choices to those that reflect long-term goals," say journalist Stephen J. Dubner and economist Steven Levitt. Commitment devices are a way to lock yourself into following a plan of action that you might not want but that you know is good for you.

Do you know it's better for you to be social than isolated? Social isolation is linked to decreased cognitive function, premature mortality rates, and poor physical health.[20] Make it easier for yourself to follow through by setting up a standing commitment. Get it on the calendar. Make it a recurring event that shows up on autopilot. Show up. Rinse, repeat. You're building habits of happiness.

What on earth do you live for, if not happiness?

Your commitments, according to Philip Brickman, an expert in the psychology of happiness. In his opinion, commitments are the true road to salvation, the solution to an otherwise absurd existence. In his work, he recognizes that commitments don't always give pleasure; they may even "oppose and conflict with freedom or happiness," as he writes in his book *Commitment, Conflict, and Caring*, but in many ways, that is the point: "The more we sacrifice for something, the more value we assign to it."

Brickman spends much of his book contemplating the pain of a commitment-less life, especially in his final chapter, "Commitment and Mental Health." Brickman argues that losing your commitments is an existential problem, robbing individuals of direction and value.[21]

A commitment device, he says, is a technique for avoiding *akrasia*, a Greek word meaning acting against one's better judgment, particularly procrastination.

Economist Jodi Beggs explains that, "Commitment devices are a way to overcome the discrepancy between an individual's short-term and long-term preferences; in other words, they are a way for self-aware people to modify their incentives or set of possible choices in order to overcome impatience or other irrational behavior." He calls the ancient story of Ulysses tying himself to the mast to avoid the sirens' lure as "the quintessential commitment device."[22]

Make it easier for yourself. *Commit*.

How to Commit

To become happy living in a digital world—using technology intentionally, for care, creativity, and community—requires the four elements of sustained change. Clarity, care, the capacity to choose wisely, and conviction about your chosen direction are essential to staying committed.[23]

Clarity

What commitments do you want to make? Remember, our goals should be specific, measurable, and time-sensitive: you define exactly what you're going to do, the terms by which you'll measure success, and the time frame in which we're going to achieve it. The closer you stick to these standards, the greater your likelihood of meaningful success. This is true of *any* plan for behavioural change.

"I'm going to improve my relationship with my partner" is a admirable sentiment, but it isn't a great goal: it's poorly defined by all of the standards above. What do you mean by *improve*? How much will you improve, and in what capacity? How will the improvement be measured?

A better example of this goal might be, "I'll spend an hour a day with my partner doing activities without our personal devices," or "I'll complete a year-long monthly couples' program with my partner," or even "I'll ask my partner how their day was every afternoon when we come together after work." Each one of these goals guides us with specific behaviour, or intention, as well as when and how often we'll do it, and under what conditions.

Will these goals improve *everything* about your relationship? Probably not by themselves, but they will undeniably improve the areas they address, and if you want to improve your relationship further, you'll set additional goals with the same clarity.

Care

To have any chance of succeeding, your goal needs to be something you care about. This is less about starting to care about things you don't, and more a reminder to be aware and honest about what you do care about.

So, do you care about the intended outcome of your goal? Why? The many voices we hear online tell us to do a lot of things—make more money, improve our health, work harder, fit more into a day—that sound like good, productive, praiseworthy things. But do they truly matter to you, or do you simply think they should? Knowing if and why a goal matters should be one of the very first steps in creating it.

Choice

A goal is a choice. It's not something you were going to do anyway, or something someone told you to do. This is important to understand because long-term goals are simply another way of framing commitments, of pledging to do what you say and continuing to do so.

Therefore, setting a goal means taking on a responsibility, a good burden, and that requires you to act with agency. It requires choice.

Your boss saying "Complete all these sales reports by Friday" isn't a goal, it's an instruction. You turn it into a goal by taking ownership of it. With clarity, you decide, *I'll complete all of these reports by the deadline*, and with care, you say, "I'm doing this because I value my job and my boss's respect in my abilities," and with choice, you say, "I accept this responsibility." Now it belongs to you—and so does the feeling of success when you achieve it.

Commitment

A long-term goal is a commitment. Just like when you engage your power to make choices, when planning a goal, you need to take into account what you're asking yourself to do: to stay with an objective, to continue working toward it, and to sustain your effort. To be in it until it's done, and maybe beyond. Just like a relationship with another human, a goal is a commitment to a set of actions and ideas. Consciously asking and answering for yourself whether you can commit to a goal and see it through is another vital step.

Accountability is part of commitment. Will you track or measure your performance to keep accountable to yourself, or will you have other people who can help keep you accountable by committing along with you or just checking in?

Commitment as a Practice

By now you understand the concept of good and bad burdens: the things we carry, whether out of choice or necessity, through life. If you're like most people today, you probably feel that you're carrying more than you're really able: you're overburdened. That may have motivated your interest in reading this book in the first place. Maybe your relationship to social media or your devices is a bad burden that's overtaken your freedom to do anything else.

> Commitments must be sustained by practice, be communal, and linked to joy —they must keep you coming back for more.

So, why all this focus on joy? When you feel low, everything feels burdensome. When you feel happy, things feel possible. This is the concept of *capacity*, whether you have the mental, emotional, and temporal space, energy, or strength to take on the commitment of a long-term goal. Committing is a self-enlarging process.[24] It builds integrity with yourself and others and shows you what you're capable of.

I am by nature a lone wolf. I'm not a joiner. I believe this hampers my progress in more ways than I can count. By observing others, experimenting with my own creative practice, and interviewing more than a hundred mindful tech leaders, I began to see a common theme: the enormous power of commitments and what's required to keep them. Over time, I learned that they must be sustained by practice, be communal, and linked to joy—they must keep you coming back for more.

Celebration Helps You Commit

Jocelyn K. Glei, host of *Hurry Slowly*, a podcast for creatives, suggests you do a little daily victory dance—offline.

Completion bias[24] wants you to finish quick tasks like checking email or scrolling through social media because they give you the sensation of progress. But it's false progress, she wisely points out. Which is what leads to digital addiction.

In RESET, her course on working better, she teaches that true motivation comes from seeing yourself make progress. She encourages students to track those "small victories" offline because digital tools too easily hide our progress. They're "almost too efficient" she says. *Intangible.* Make tracking physical and visible to make progress obvious. Then, when you do complete a milestone, get off your chair and do a little dance.

Shake it with me.

(If you're not a dancer, give yourself a gold star sticker or high five. They work, I promise.)

Combining Joys Helps You Commit

In 2020, Erin Peace began running. As a design director in New York City, technology is both a vital tool in her work and also the subject of every project. Like you, she struggles with digital burnout, facing tech challenges in both her personal and professional life.

"I work in tech and now I work remotely in tech. Just hacking the tools to make them fit my needs would be my biggest professional challenge," she says.

> Sometimes I can't do that in a way that is sustainable, given the fact that my work is highly collaborative. The only way I currently see my colleagues is through digital

technology. So, there's a trap there that I can't escape. But when I say hacking, I mean, just like making sure I'm going into the settings and turning off notifications for all the things that aren't really relevant, staying off social media during work, all of those kinds of things.

Her biggest challenge is transitioning from work productivity to what she wants to do offline, whether it's cooking, running, reading, or just talking to her partner.

"It's not the fault of my job, but the nature of working on screens all day," she says. "It's a very reactive environment. To try and transition is a huge mindset shift. I had to build practices in like a mile walk every morning or getting outside the minute that work ends."

Committing to the practice of walking was pivotal for Erin. It's changed the way she shows up in the world.

"I've realized that when I don't have [these walks], I am significantly more anxious. I sleep worse. I think it's because when I go to sleep thinking that I just have to wake up and turn on the computer, it's a very stressful way to fall asleep. Whereas getting outside and moving is a little bit of something to look forward to in the morning."

On her daily walk, she leaves her phone at home.

"I live right next to Prospect Park so I am lucky that I just get to be in nature, but it's a very, very simple thing. Just the habit of it has really helped me."

Walking turned to running. Erin recently ran her first marathon. She took up this commitment during the COVID-19 pandemic.

"I think I began now because what else was I going to focus on?" she says. She joined a community of people that meet to run together. "Having the endorphins of community, exercise, and nature, all in one, and a goal I was working toward, I think was probably the biggest tool that helped me get through the year without feeling too depressed or anxious."

This commitment has led Erin to a new one:

> I want to pay more attention in everything I do. I learned that from Ellen Langer when she explains how mindfulness is not meditating, but it is noticing new things. I've really taken that to heart because I'm very much a planner—thinking about my next trip, what I want in my career, things like that. But, lately, there's been so much I couldn't plan for. I had to really focus on the here and now. Make it interesting, right? Make my breakfast interesting.
>
> I want to commit to furthering that skill of paying attention to my daily life and really learning what I enjoy and what I want to devote my time and attention to.

That is a worthy goal. A commitment in reach of all of us. The only way to become committed is to commit.

Let us be the ones who build communities;
who know each other's names.

Quests

1. Find and join one social or volunteer club or organization that meets regularly, whether virtually or in person. (*Need help choosing? Answer this: The three interests I have that I'd most like to share with other people are…*)

2. Create at least one standing social commitment each week. (*Answer this: The three people I'd most like to improve or deepen my relationship through a standing social commitment are…*)

3. Stay committed. To be committed is to be generous. No more cancelling, no more excuses. Be impeccable with your word. It's a good burden.

The goal is aliveness.
The purpose is love.

Take up the good burden of being committed.

IV

REALIGNING WITH JOY

Connection is shrinking the distance between people.
—Pamela Pavliscak

I remember the day my middle school teachers invited me to be a sanctuary.

I'd come from a small private elementary school in suburban Vancouver. It was across the street from my church, a place as familiar to me and my brothers and sisters as our comfortable middle-class home. When I came to the end of seventh grade, my mom chose an inner-city school for me on Vancouver's Eastside. It was a private school with tuition, but it also had a generous pay structure that supported lower-income-family enrollment. It supported the education of kids not like me. Kids I didn't even know existed. My school was, in fact, a haven for kids no longer welcome in the public school system—who'd been kicked out too many times.

This is where I met Tia.

Tia was like no girl I'd ever met. Bold and loud, with thick, wiry hair and a take-no-prisoners attitude that drew me in like a moth to a flame. We were instant best friends.

I remember the first time I visited Tia's house. It was tucked behind a Dairy Queen on a busy crosstown thoroughfare. Her home was in a co-op, two floors high, attached to a hundred other homes exactly like hers. She lived there with her mom and little sister, Cordelaine—both tough as nails. Their tiny kitchen had just enough room for a fridge, oven, microwave, and three-foot countertop—just enough room for us to squeeze in, in search of after-school snacks. In this neighbourhood, kids taught us how to say dirty words in Filipino. We weren't in suburbia anymore.

One day, a few months into my second year of middle school, my teachers sat me down for a special meeting. I couldn't figure out why I was there. I wasn't a kid who got into trouble. I sat, curious, across from Mr. T (Mr. Tigchelaar, my homeroom teacher; the one who let us keep a set of dirty clothes in our gym lockers just in case of perfect muddy tackle-football weather).

Three teachers sat across from me in my empty grade 9 class-room and told me that Tia's mom was in intensive care because she had attempted suicide.

Those teachers sat there and told me that my friend needed me. They knew she'd need me for a while. They told me I could have at least three weeks off of school to do whatever needed doing. To be there for my friend. To offer her space, time, to *be a sanctuary* for her as she visited her mom, took care of her little sister, and began the process of grieving, healing, and making sense of this terrible, terrible thing.

I remember them, these teachers, men and women I looked up to, saying, "You need to be with your friend. Go."

So, I went.

Being a Sanctuary

This is first time I remember being a sanctuary, a place of refuge, for someone outside my own family. A time when I had to choose to leave my comfortable cocoon of self-indulgence and respond to someone's heart saying, *I don't know what I need right now, but would you please just be here with me?*

To *give refuge* is to shelter or protect from danger or distress—to provide safe harbour from the storm. So, I sat with Tia in her pain. Her mom recovered. And none of us were ever the same.

I carry this knowledge of sanctuary with me to this day. I believe it is possible, in our hyper-connected world, to offer sanc-tuary, experiences of total rest and acceptance, to a weary world. I believe we can wrest back control from the dominating technol-ogies that pull us out of a place of presence and cultivate places of refuge and connection in our day-to-day lives.

Throughout this book, you've begun discovering and being led by your joys—taking up the good burdens of being here and awake, human and you, useful and committed. In this sec-tion, you will learn how to realign with your joys in the months and years to come by cultivating gratitude and honing courage. Realigning with Joy requires flexibility and focus, being attentive to the opportunities and obstacles coming your way.

Throughout your life, you will encounter opportunities to expand your capacity, to embrace new experiences, and respond to circumstances demanding more from you than ever before. Each time, a choice must be made: to stay the course, or set a new one.

To courageously navigate uncharted waters and carry a more substantial burden, you will need to refit the ship that is you.

Refitting and Course Correcting

Refitting and course correcting are the longest stages of our lives because they are the parts that challenge us to begin again and again. Ships are never made for a single journey; they are too expensive, time-consuming, and passionate an undertaking to be used just once and cast aside. Ships are built to last, and if we are fortunate, our lives will consist of many voyages.

The United States Navy is far and away the most powerful and modern naval force in the world, but one of its ships, the USS *Blue Ridge*, its oldest operational vessel, is currently a little over fifty years old—in service longer than many of us!

How can this be? Ships that remain seaworthy, healthy enough to keep going, and valuable enough to be considered worth the expense, are regularly refitted. *Blue Ridge* was built in 1967 and launched in 1970, decades before the existence of the internet, but today she's a command, control, and intelligence ship serving in the Sea of Japan, carrying some of the most sophisticated computers and electronics in the Navy.

If we want to remain seaworthy, we must examine our own kit often. What needs to be discarded? What needs maintenance or updating? What new things can we take on to make us faster, steadier, or stronger? A well-designed ship carries only what it needs, and nothing more.

Another part of the ongoing lives of ships is course correction. As many of us probably learned, or will learn, in our first voyages going just one degree off our intended course takes us farther and farther from our goal the longer we travel.

If you've ever been aboard a ship, or observed one as it moves through the water, you know that "steering" is only part of it. Objects as big as ships, moving through a dynamic fluid far bigger than themselves, don't turn corners, spin out, or slam on the brakes to avoid colliding with hazards. Every major change in direction requires advanced planning, skill, and allowances for time. That's the difference between steering and navigating.

You are the ship. Or, to be precise, the ship is your life: who you are, where you've been, and where you're going. If *steering* the ship is making small, daily decisions like deciding what to eat for lunch, what outfit to wear to a party, what television show to watch next, *navigating* involves more substantive choices like deciding on a healthy diet, building a wardrobe that fits your budget, or shaping your viewing habits to include a range of positive activities.

Navigation requires knowledge and forethought. It isn't just spinning a wheel—though the wheel, our small, daily choices, is part of it.

Here's something interesting to consider while we're talking about navigation. The ancient Greek word for navigate, *kuber*, is where we get the word cybernetics, *kubern tikós*, meaning an intelligent system of control. In the English language, the prefix "cyber" has evolved, of course, to mean anything chiefly happening online. Cyberbullying. Cyberethics. Cybercrime. It is ironic that a word fundamentally meaning the *control* of something large and powerful has evolved to refer mainly to things that we often feel we have no control over.

Do you feel like *you* have control over cyberspace?

You are here because you're striving to be a better navigator of this digital age: to know where you should go and how to get there. It's a skill of lifelong learning, with increasing returns and rewards, allowing you to seek more distant, ambitious shores with confidence and ability.

A successful voyage means knowing your ship, knowing the sea, and knowing the way you want to go.

Be Grateful

Slow down.
Pay attention.
Do good work.
Love your neighbour.
Love your place.
Stay in your place.
Settle for less, enjoy it more.
—Wendell Berry

The process of communication involves exchange, back and forth. It's what much of our current communication is lacking: why calling someone and getting their voice mail, texting instead of talking, or posting updates online can feel flat. I was feeling this flatness a few years ago.

I had just watched a documentary featuring a scene where a priest conducts a blessing service for smartphones. Here was a person, dressed in holy vestments, calling on the God of the Universe to bless a BlackBerry (remember those?). Blessing actual blackberries, harvested for our bodies' use, would have been one thing, but blessing a smartphone—a piece of glass, metal, and plastic designed to accelerate our lives to the brink of exhaustion—was quite another. I found myself looking at the phone constantly in my hand, asking: Could this thing be a blessing? Could it be blessed?

It was a time in my life where I'd grown tired of the web mediating my relationships. I felt the distance between myself and others growing. The internet, I believed, was making me lazy as a thinker, a writer, and a friend. I wasn't engaging in the effort of remembering things or reaching out to spend time with family and friends the way I used to. As a student of media theory, I knew I was, to borrow a term from Neil Postman, "amusing myself to death": allowing myself to emotionally disengage whole gorging on mundane online filler.

One day, I woke up with the idea to give the internet up for a month. I wanted discover what kind of person, parent, and artist I could and would be offline.

Why was I in such a hurry? What was I gaining through my online check-ins? Why was I turning down in-person get-togethers? These were some of the questions I set out to explore. The plan took shape over the course of a few months. Preparations included buying a map book, writing down important phone numbers I had a tendency to google, and notifying freelance clients. To chronicle my journey, I decided to write one letter a day on my Remington typewriter and mail it to a friend. Thirty-one days, thirty-one letters from a Luddite. Nervous and excited, I set up my auto-responder and pulled the plug.

As with any detox, the first few days were bumpy. I responded to phantom vibrations from my phone, realized just how much I relied on Google, and spent a lot of time wondering what was happening online—especially on the website about my experiment I'd (ironically) set up.

But the urge to control quickly gave way to joy.

There was nothing I could do about it. I was free.

During those thirty-one days, I discovered an abundance of time I never thought I had. I experienced peace, a quietness of mind I had been hungering for. I found connection with neighbours, strangers, and friends because I was forced to turn to people rather than to Google for help. I was figuring out how to flourish in a never-off culture. I was experiencing the joy of missing out—the conscious choice to unplug and experience life offline.

There are many voices calling to us, keeping us from a place of rest and refuge; many commitments reducing our margin to experience and offer sanctuary. It's because we are living in a world where the speed and gloss of our screens often make the connection to those far away seem more interesting and urgent than the world, and people, right in front of us. It's happening to teens at prom, CEOs in boardrooms, kids and teachers in classrooms, and daily to you and me. These technologies tap into novelty and the very human longing for connection. We want to know what's happening. We want to connect, and we don't want to miss out. Unlike the longer-lasting happiness we experience connecting in the real world, short-term, dopamine-driven feedback loops hook us into shallow engagement online.[26] We're stuck treading water at the surface level of our lives.

> We're stuck treading water at the surface level of our lives.

What has our hyper-connectivity really given us?

After *The Joy of Missing Out*, the book based on my internet fast, was published, *Women's Health* magazine asked me to comment on a rising phenomenon (with its expected catchy acronym) called FOGO, the Fear Of Going Out. They explained that mental health experts were concerned by a growing number of people expressing anxiety about engaging in social activities outside of the home—citing the lack of energy to be "on," not having a set end time for an evening out, and even wondering whether people really want them at the party or event. Social anxiety is a real phobia, and it's growing. So it seems like now, instead of scrolling through our social media feeds and feeling jealous or lonely—what's commonly referred to FOMO, or Fear Of Missing Out, which we explored in Section I—we're feeling some dread and anxiety even when we're explicitly *invited* out.

I told the writer at *Women's Health* that this makes sense because our online environments are controlled while the world, and the humans living in it, is intrinsically unpredictable.

So, we're not going out because we're fearful of the real world and we are stuck online because we're scared of missing out on it.

The result is that our energies, creativity, and time—perhaps the best of us—is being spent on screens. It's also resulting in staggering levels of loneliness and isolation, which have only been exacerbated by the stay-at-home orders of the global COVID-19 pandemic.

Of all age groups, Generation Z (those born in the mid- to late '90s to the early 2010s) have been particularly impacted. According to a study by the global health service company Cigna, Gen Z is significantly more likely than any other age group to say they experience feelings associated with loneliness; 69 percent say they feel like "no one really knows them well."[26]

On top of all that, the advertising ecosystem we've grown up in has told us that the most important thing in the world is our personal pleasure and ease, with no concern for the consequences. The closed grid of the internet has helped us forget the world is outside the edges.

Our technologies may be changing at breakneck speed, and we may now measure data in Yodabytes (yes, it's a thing), but one thing remains.

Our human hearts are still saying, *Just be here with me.*

Our need for belonging remains.

Finding Meaning in Moments

I am not a weaver, but I have a particular love for the fibre arts, especially felting. There is something about the forgiveness of wool, its softness, and the ways it reminds me of the natural world. That love deepened when my sister-in-law surprised me with a felt-garland-making workshop near her home in Hood River, Oregon. On a summer evening, we gathered around a long table in an open, street-level studio. In front of each participant lay a few piles of dyed wool, a long sharp pin, and a square piece of foam. These were all the supplies, I was told, I'd need in order to walk home with a string of colourful felt balls.

Two things to know about me: I'm not particularly patient, and (related) I have little tolerance for fiddly things. I was born with brachydactyly type D, better known as "toe thumbs," so I have bulbous appendages that make things like texting on tiny screens or threading needles a nightmare. (Fun fact: my thumbs also have a tendency to get stuck in bowling balls.) So, this craft was right up my alley: take wool, roll it into ball, attack with pin. This, I could do.

I was the first to draw blood. Ball after ball, Band-Aid after Band-Aid, my felt garland took shape. The group chattered and laughed; we paused to admire each other's creations and make suggestions. In all, the workshop lasted ninety minutes. We'd all made something beautiful: a garland, a friend, a memory.

I have often thought of the work of relationship like weaving. Less like the loom, mechanical and repetitive, and more like the spider. The spinning of the web, the interlocking threads, the magical display when all is said and done. No web is ever the same but always, there is beauty.

The Web You Weave

It's February and I take my kids out sledding. We drive to a nearby hill with a sizeable slope—bigger and better than our local park's—covered in a thin dusting of snow. The kids run ahead, toboggans in tow, while I take up the rear, chatting on the phone with my husband, Michael, who is at home working. After a few minutes, I wander over to get eyes on the kids when I spot Caleb, our youngest, lying at the bottom of the hill, his older brother and an adult beside. My first thought is that there's been a collision between mine and this stranger's kid and I prepare to make apologies. I awkwardly scramble down the icy stairs to the base of the hill, where I'm in for a shock.

My son, I am told by the generous stranger, barrelled straight into the metal railing that cuts through the centre of the hill. The dad, Alain, who saw the whole thing happen, says he hit the pole near the bottom of the hill at top speed, got up, and teetered around, before collapsing on the ground.

I turn to my son, splayed out on the ice in his navy one-piece snowsuit, slowly turning his own shade of blue. He shivers silently as I ask him what happened, where it hurts, and if I can carry him to our vehicle. He gives little reply, suddenly drifting in and out of consciousness. I scream him awake, every ounce of my old lifeguard training coursing through my body.

Do not let him close his eyes. Do not let him fall unconscious.

After minutes of weighing my options, I point-blank ask Alain, who's been suggesting paramedics from the start: "If this was your kid, would you be calling 911?"

"Yes," he says. "Better safe than sorry."

The paramedics arrive and take Caleb to the closest emergency room. They quickly transfer him to SickKids hospital for what ends up being a seven-day stay to heal from the internal bleeding from his nearly ruptured kidney.

As we're settling our family of five into two camps, Hospital and Home, and the evolving mess of logistics of caring for someone hospitalized during a pandemic, the web emerges.

> *Word spreads. Offers of help flood our phones. Check-ins. Are you ok?s. Thinking of you. Prayers. Day after day, meals arriving on the doorstep. No more room in the fridge. Piles of handwritten cards delivered to our door by our public school teachers. Call after call. Caleb's second-grade teacher, Ms. Masellas, catches me on her lunch break the day after we arrive at the hospital. The vulnerability and awkwardness of us both trying to comfort one another. Suddenly, finally, the tremble in her voice breaks me right open. For the pain and fear for my son but also the tender bravery of her calling. We wait out the tears, together. She's shrunk the distance between us. Somehow now forever closer.*

After 168 hours of pokes, prods, and pain meds, Caleb and I cuddle up on his hospital bed to watch the movie *Inside Out*. We listen together as Joy finally realizes "They came to help because of sadness."

Never before have I been so grateful for my neighbours and the investment we have made in our community. The invisible web we'd been weaving for years, now suddenly visible.

The Benefits of Belonging

Every year, our family hosts a pumpkin-carving party in our Toronto neighbourhood. We buy a mess of pumpkins and deliver handmade flyers. The first year, we had no idea how many people would show up. We hung a poster from our corner-lot hedge for a couple of weeks with a few details:

> *Join us for a Neighbourhood Pumpkin Carving Party*
> *Pumpkins, refreshments, and good times provided*

Sprinkle in some rudimentary pumpkin-face drawings and jagged Sharpie lettering and you get the idea.

The big day rolled around and we set up a smattering of borrowed fold-out tables, secured helium balloons to the shrubbery, and rolled out the massive pile of pumpkins we'd stashed in our garage.

Seventy-five people showed up.

A steady stream of families, couples, and singles, young and old, who had seen the sign, heard through the grapevine, or were simply out walking and saw the festivities. Some stayed for hours; others came by with gift baskets to send their regrets—they had other plans—but to tell us they were so happy we were doing this. My industrious friend Adrienne, a clothing designer who likes to be busy with her hands, took it upon herself to create a pumpkin-gut sorting centre so we could offer people bags of pumpkin seeds to roast at home.

Soon, we became known as the pumpkin-carving family. We'd have it no other way.

We've committed to this neighbourhood for more than a decade, since we moved from Vancouver when our first child, Madeleine, was one. When it was our moment of need, the community rose up and carried us.

Why am I telling you all of this?

Because it's in these small but impactful ways that we create community over time. Pumpkin carving was something our family could deliver on. It made us feel good. Proud. Like we were contributing something lasting and real to our neighbours. It was small but it was something. And our neighbours found community there with each other, and with us.

There are so many benefits to belonging. Choose to be a weaver. With each interlocking string, you're building a web that will catch you when you fall.

Won't You Be My Neighbour?

I jump on my powder blue bike and cycle over to our local community-run theatre to meet my friend Kristy for the Mr. Rogers documentary, the sun silently slipping behind me. Friendship. Film. Forward motion. All the good of summer rolled into one night.

The film tells the story of Fred Rogers, a soft-spoken would-be pastor who found a different calling, providing an oasis for children in a sea of televised violence. I learn how the landmark series I grew up on, *Mister Rogers' Neighborhood*, gently delved into important subjects, like desegregation and war, that no other children's show dared to discuss at the time.

I listen to Fred Rogers say, "The greatest thing that we can do is to help somebody know that they're loved and capable of loving...I believe that when we look for what's best in a person we happen to be with at the moment, we're doing what God does all the time. So in loving and appreciating our neighbor, we're participating in something sacred."

In moments like these, I drop my popcorn and lunge for Kristy's hand, my tear-filled eyes silently asking her, *Are you hearing this? Are you hearing these words? Do you hear what he's saying?*

Our world has changed, yes. But the greatest things, the essential things, haven't.

Kristy is my neighbour. She serves on the board of the community-run theatre we're sitting in. She and I once co-hosted a

What is the last social interaction that felt sacred to you, and why?

sold-out documentary event in this space. This is our place; these are our people.

Won't you be my neighbour?

The next morning, I pick up Brené Brown's *Braving the Wilderness*, where she writes about the essentialness of neighbours, people to share our sorrows and joys with, face to face.

"Being alone in the midst of a widely reported trauma, watching endless hours of twenty-four-hour news or reading countless articles on the Internet, is the quickest way for anxiety and fear to tiptoe into your heart and plant their roots of secondary trauma," she writes about her own experience with the Sandy Hook Elementary School shootings back in 2012. She chose to cry with her friends before heading to church to cry with strangers.

Moments of collective joy and pain are sacred experiences.

"They are so deeply human that they cut through our differences and tap into our hardwired nature. These experiences tell us what is true and possible about the human spirit," says Brené. She suggests that these moments are necessary reminders that no matter whether we like someone or not—on- or offline—"we are still inextricably connected." And it doesn't have to be a major or life-altering event; it can be something as simple as speaking to the person sitting next to us on a flight.

Good Burdens

Mr. Rogers spent his whole life closing that gap. In loving and appreciating our neighbour, even in relying on them in hard times, he said, we are participating in something vital. It took me a long time to see that our gifts are as true as our griefs. We all have something to offer.

After the movie, Kristy and I settle on a side street bench to catch up on six months of life. We talk about marriage and missed opportunities, whether or not I should dye my hair platinum (*You should do it!* she shouts. And I do.) We talk about the city shooting that happened across town, just outside her workplace, and the reverberations she, her co-workers, and the neighbourhood are experiencing. We talk past dark and hug goodbye before I pedal home in the still night.

This night felt sacred. It felt like a gift.

Have you known moments like this?

Gratitude is Joy, Witnessed

If you stop and take a moment to let them in, you'll see that joys abound.

When you begin looking into, listing, and living your joys, listlessness and lethargy retreat. That's because you beat scarcity—the feeling you never have enough—with gratitude.

Research shows very clearly that people who engage in active gratitude, meaning reflection on their success and its sources, are less vulnerable to depression and more able to access empathy and connect to the people they lead, love, and live with.

The habit of keeping a gratitude list (which—surprise!—you have already begun with your 100 Joys) has innumerable benefits. Studies have shown that those who prioritize this practice have a relative absence of stress and depression, make progress toward important personal goals, report higher levels of determination and energy, feel closer in their relationships and desire to build stronger ones, and increase happiness by 25 percent.[28]

Who wouldn't want a quarter more happiness?

Resist for Reward

To grow in gratitude and its accompanying joys, you must resist one mighty enemy: the age-old vice of acedia. Acedia is a combination of apathy and boredom. To me, it means being checked out, not noticing, deadened, dull.

It's resistance to the demands of love.[29]

Resist acedia. Resist for your reward. Remember: the goal is aliveness, the purpose is love.

And love is a good burden.

Gratitude, then, is the *measuring* part in measurable. It's about pausing to examine our well-being and successes—the elements of joy—to evaluate where they come from and celebrate them.

> We're wired for gratitude, just as we're wired for joy.

You're pausing right now to read this book. Take a few minutes to consider and celebrate the good fortune, supportive families, friends, mentors, and natural talents it took to create the perfect storm for you to arrive at this moment, to have already achieved so much in so many ways. Because we're wired for gratitude, just as we're wired for joy.

Weave your web.

*Let us be the ones who are grateful for what we have;
who waste no thought on what we don't need.*

Quests

1. Think of a good burden in your life. How can you recommit to it today?

2. Introduce 20 more joys to your growing list on page 166.

3. Learn the name of one new neighbour and draw a simple neighbourhood map to help you remember. We all want to be known by name.

*The goal is aliveness.
The purpose is love.*

Take up the good burden of being grateful.

Be Brave

If I affirm that the universe was created by a power of love,
and that all creation is good, I am not proclaiming safety.
Safety was never part of the promise.
Creativity, yes; safety, no.
—Madeleine L'Engle, *And It Was Good*

In the treetops of Fewell Island, South Carolina, six young adults in harnesses dangle awkwardly from ropes. Down below, a group stands huddled in windbreakers and hoodies in the frigid February air, calling out encouragement to the Irish girl tearfully facing her fears twenty feet overhead.

"Come on, Paula! You've got this!"

Forty minutes later, a crowd greets Paula with triumphant cheers as she zip-lines her way back to solid ground. Our group's easy camaraderie belies the fact that most of us have met less than twenty-four hours ago. We are here for a digital detox retreat—each of us voluntarily without phones. Most of the attendees, ironically, found out about the retreat on social media. Paula McKee, of high-ropes-course fame, an au pair from Belfast, was invited by text.

We all braved showing up.

The internet has helped foster these kinds of trusting acts. For example, finding a one-person, independent operation online and booking with them, trusting their credentials and promises, and then showing up! Trust has also powered the growth of the sharing economy.

While the debate rages on whether this so-called gig economy is undermining secure jobs by replacing them with an army of mercenary, part-time workers, it has opened up new avenues of trust and camaraderie between citizens as they become customer and client. You're dealing with gig workers every day. The gig economy is a labour market characterized by the prevalence of short-term contracts or freelance work as opposed to permanent jobs.

The traditional commercial relationship, too, becomes more complex in the gig economy. Instead of grunting a rote "How are you today?" or "Have a nice day" or other platitudes as we do at retail outlets, we want to know more about the person we've contracted before we accept their services or rate them. That's opening up intimate conversations most consumers have never had to have before, which in turn opens up all types of opportunities to network, trust, and share, ultimately creating an opportunity for relationships.

Ten years ago, for example, no one would have dreamed of getting into the back of a stranger's car or staying in their apartment. Now, thanks to Airbnb and car services like Lyft and Uber, it's commonplace. (The Anabaptists, cool kids that they are, were doing their version of Airbnb, called Mennonite Your Way, long before the internet.)

Trust is built, and broken, the same way online and off: through the keeping or severing of promises. While trust can begin to grow online, it is solidified in close physical proximity. That's why when we meet our ride-share driver, our trust in them and the sharing economy grows. We've closed the gap.

Of course, this trust can be broken in stunning ways; the internet, through people's use of blatant visual distortion and propagation of misinformation, provides plenty of opportunities for this. Trusting communities require a balance between nurturing existing relationships and extending outward to form new ones. Mistrust can grow when communities only take care of "their own."

Living Hope

Chris Lawrence is a pastor of the Church of the Living Hope in New York City's East Harlem, an English-speaking congregation in a historically Spanish community. His church members are making progress slowly with what they call "re-neighbouring the street": connecting four hundred households that share the same block but do not currently have much to do with each other.

"Although lots of them are on their phones a great deal, wired into the cyber relationships that beckon to them," says Lawrence, "we are focusing efforts on creating a 'people-friendly urban village' on our block."

Those efforts include an annual, block-long "De Colores" street feast, during which a congregant who is an *Elle* magazine photographer takes family portraits. Another program pairs teens with elderly neighbours to help them buy Christmas gifts for their grandchildren online. The church's mission is to reclaim the trust they feel has been lost over the last twenty years—both due to the isolation the internet has wrought as well as language barriers the church feels they have helped perpetuate by not providing enough services in Spanish—by focusing outward.

While these efforts are primarily embodied through the hard work of the individuals in the neighbourhood and their active efforts, Living Hope is also working with local technologists to build an app for the immediate neighbourhood.

"It will be entirely bilingual and needs to touch the demographic of local low-income households and not just mimic the platforms frequented by gentrifiers such as the Nextdoor app," says Lawrence. While Nextdoor was intended as a hyperlocal neighbourhood social networking service, it has been widely criticized for facilitating nasty gossip from upwardly mobile users seeking to weed out "problem" neighbours and businesses.

Ultimately, Lawrence said, the goal is to get people offline and into each other's lives, where lasting trust can be built. "I'm aware that in our neighbourhood we need to work at every level, including the internet, to get people to be more comfortable sharing their lives and stories and being curious with who lives on the same street," said Lawrence. "It is incredibly important."

How we build trust in a digital age *is* of utmost importance. We can't know our neighbours at arms' length, and we can't expect to form community if we remain strangers to each other. The model that the sharing economy has created over the past decade might show us the way to connect. In a very practical sense, when we have positive, trusting encounters, it gives our hearts the courage to trust more.

As we choose to trust each other more and that trust is reciprocated, our trust is strengthened. This helps us build trusting relationships—the bedrock of thriving families, communities, neighbourhoods, and nations. You can't build trust without first trusting.

> When we have positive, trusting encounters, it gives our hearts the courage to trust more.

And it seems we're finally starting to get it: in an age of unprecedented mistrust, the sharing economy, based on mutual trust, is thriving.

What kind of world do we want to live in?

Surely, it's a culture of loving trust. It's a world worth making.

Hone Courage

There is vital importance in taking risks and trying new things. But we're afraid. And it's stopping us from living our lives fully. As Arthur Brooks writes in *The Atlantic*, "Fear of failure can have surprisingly harsh consequences for our well-being."[30] It can, he explains, lead to "debilitating anxiety and depression, a diagnosable malady called atychiphobia," the definition of which is literally "an irrational and persistent fear of failing." But even if it doesn't reach that crisis point, he warns, "it can steer us away from life's joyful, fulfilling adventures, by discouraging us from taking risks and trying new things."

The most surprising part? The solution, Brooks explains, is not to "extinguish the fear itself" to become "fearless," but to tame it. How do you do so? One simple word.

Courage.

Like our brave friend Paula.

For many of us, the first hurdle is honing the courage to take up the burden of the real world. No longer using the internet to hide. Removing barriers to our feelings by avoiding avoidance. We can hide by being quiet or loud, showing all of ourselves or nothing at all—any online action motivated by shame or fostering smallness. Hiding is showing the shadow self.

"I knew I wasn't loved online," says Lana, my internet-turned-real-life-friend. "I was addicted and felt lousy most of the time. I saw continual reminders that I'm not enough. Not pretty enough. Not cool enough. Not funny enough. Not inspirational enough."

She recently reached out to tell me she's been taking a lot of time off social media, gushing, "I didn't realize how freeing it was."

"Keep going," I tell her.

How do we hone courage?

We do it in community, not in isolation. Where is your community, and does it bring you joy? It takes courage to form real relationships.

Joy matters to your relationship with the online world. Why? The path to joy is not effortless, it's effortful. It's not mindless, it's mindful. It requires courage.

The time you spend online and what you consume there is most often designed to be effortlessly convenient and abundant, thoughtless and unintentional, and ultimately in service of someone else's values and goals, not your own. Algorithms measure the known, not the possible. Content curated to your past behaviour doesn't challenge your curiosity or courage. Content served up binge-style, ready-made in endless quantities with more always on the way, asks no effort from us.

Experiencing joy takes work. Consuming doesn't.

Algorithms measure the known, not the possible.

Not only is joy not effortless, it isn't frivolous, either. In order to prioritize your joy, you need to develop a positive relationship with your abilities *and* your limits when it comes to accomplishing your goals. You will need to be brave. It is courageous to connect to your true desires and to accept your unique capacities. None of us is the same.

I want to make something perfectly clear here. You only *get* brave by surrounding yourself with and taking on board the voices that build you up. That's how you build the courage to live joyfully in the digital age.

Be Intentional

In my senior year of high school (way back in the glorious late '90s,) a guy named Matt made it his mission to taunt me with a bizarre nickname: Goat. When I confronted him, he told me the choice was completely random, but his persistence made it catch on. Within weeks, more than a dozen seventeen- and eighteen-year-old boys were herding around me, bleating, *meh-heh-heh-heh*. Over and over again.

I grew up with a gaggle of brothers, which gave me an unhealthy level of tolerance for this behaviour. To be honest, to a certain extent I liked the (albeit tasteless) attention. I was a popular athlete, not a shy wallflower. Still, Goat got to me. It was a diminishment I allowed

Imagine your ideal community. What part do you play?

for too long. I last heard the bleating at graduation, climbing the stairs to the stage to receive a scholarship for best all-around athlete.

Turns out the joke's on him. I am the GOAT. *Greatest of All Time.*

It's shocking that any of us would consciously put ourselves in the way of voices or images that diminish us, but it's what we do every time we mindlessly scroll social media.

Do you *need* to feel this way? No. So, it's time to get intentional.

Intentionality is one of the key principles of living joyfully. It basically means that we don't do anything unless we're doing it deliberately. Consistent intentionality takes work—especially when it comes to our digital lives. You've already taken an intentional step by reading this book.

You now understand how your media environment is contributing to your FOMO, creating and sustaining the narrative that you can't keep up. Hopefully, you've begun turning down the volume on your digital life, getting rid of the extra voices that don't serve you, so you can enjoy more daily presence and peace. You are discovering your joys and beginning to see how prioritizing the people and pastimes you love fills you up.

Well done. Now the question is, how are you going to make these changes stick?

The following principles I've developed, along with regular digital house-cleaning, will help you stay on track.

The 4 Principles of Digital Well-Being

1. NOMO FOMO

Remember FOMO's core messages? *You don't have enough. You aren't doing enough. You are not enough.* Pay attention to the sources of these voices and regularly eliminate them.

2. Consistently Cull

The sheer volume of information you're expected to process on a daily basis makes it difficult to focus on what matters. To control your digital consumption, regularly cull your accounts. I call this digital house-cleaning. Every month, follow these steps:

Social Media Unfollow: Pick 1 social media platform and unfollow 20 accounts. Ask yourself: *Who is this? Does it feel good, or is it important? Do I want to bring this with me?* If the answer is no, say goodbye.

Email Unsubscribe: Spend 10 minutes unsubscribing from email newsletters. (Unroll.me is an excellent free resource for this.) Ask yourself: *Who is this? Does it feel good or is it important? Do I want to bring this with me?* If the answer is no, unsubscribe.

Desktop and Browser Tidy: Organize your files and bookmarks into two categories, *Important Documents* and *Spark Joy*. If an item doesn't belong in either folder, pull it into the trash and say goodbye.

Phone Tidy: Delete any apps you haven't used in the last month and keep time-wasting apps in a creatively named folder like *Are you sure?* at least one swipe away from the home screen. Better yet, delete them.

3. Peaceful Progress

You have ambitious goals and deep desires for connection. Your digital use has the capacity to help or hinder your progress. When we break things down into achievable pieces, we achieve our goals, gaining momentum, confidence, and hope. Focus on short-term wins like completing the digital house-cleaning each month or unfollowing even just one account that longer serves you. Peaceful progress is the key. You're doing great.

4. Toward the Life-Giving

I believe the key to thriving with technology is less about limiting screen time and more about creating the positive conditions for other, more life-giving engagements to flourish. Your new daily practice of asking: *What today was most life-giving / life-taking?* will, over time, orient you toward the life-giving, helping you overcome digital overwhelm, do your best work, and experience more joy.

Remember, you are the ship. You deserve to feel magnificent, confident in your chosen direction, consistently offloading cargo that's holding you back. Good burdens aboard only.

My friend Lana is a strong, beautiful riot of a human being. I want to kick at any voice that tears her down. Is quitting social media a step forward for her? Yes. *It's unhealthy to deeply love anything that cannot love you back*, I gently remind her.

There is a better way forward, though. That's what this section is all about. Because, as my friend, Kevan Gilbert, Facilitation Practice Lead at digital transformation agency Domain7, reminds me, social media, and all of the internet, can be a tool for good.

He tells me: "I've been overjoyed and humbled at the ways I've been healing and learning thanks to the help of Instagram accounts powered by people who share their stories and their professional insights. These leaders and communicators bring tears to my eyes with their bravery and honesty and healing and humour!"

You can love the internet, but the internet can't love you back. Only people can. And what is the internet? It's a web of people. The right people can help you be brave.

Being You is Brave

To write this book, I need courage, so I make regular visits to a statue of writer Lesya Ukrainka in High Park, a short bike ride from my house. I bring her little offerings: notes, flowers, a beaded necklace on a string. The monument, which I happened upon quite accidentally one day, was erected in 1975 and is engraved with Lesya's words: "Whoever liberates themselves shall be free. Whoever is liberated by others captive shall remain."

Over time I learn that Lesya Ukrainka is the pen name of Ukranian writer Larissa Kosach. As the plaque in her honour reads, "Undaunted by a debilitating lifelong illness, she created a rich legacy, writing about recurring themes like the relationship of the individual to the community, the role of women in society, human dignity, and the writer as a force for betterment."

The writer as a force for betterment.

Yes. These are the words I hold onto. Over time, they become the meditation of my heart.

Dear Lesya, I scribble, *I know that for you to have said so much, you feared little. Pray for me. That I may love much and my fear dissolve in its embrace.*

I fold up the square piece of origami paper and tuck it in the wooden fence.

My friend Ted wrote a book called *The Uber of Everything* at a time when every Silicon Valley–bound start-up was calling themselves the Uber of something. The Uber of Swimming Pools, The Uber of Car Rentals, The Uber of Snow Removal, The Uber of *Whatever.*

My advice to you? Be the Uber of Nothing.

Don't worry about being everything to everyone. Focus on the relationships in your life that are good burdens. That are worth the effort.

Hone courage. Be you. Be brave.

Let us be the ones who are courageous;
who choose adventure over regret.

You can have control or you can have growth. Which do you choose?

Quests

1. Write down the 4 Principles of Digital Well-being—NOMO FOMO, Consistently Cull, Peaceful Progress, Toward the Life-giving—and place them near your computer.

2. Answer: how will I surround myself with voices that help me hone courage?

3. Add 20 more joys to your list.

The goal is aliveness.
The purpose is love.

Take up the good burden of being brave.

V

ADOPTING FOR JOY

Joy—it's not just a gift. In a sense it's also a duty,
a task to fulfill. Courage.
—Anna Kamienska, *Astonishments*

So, here you are. How are you feeling? I hope inside you is a growing desire to take up good burdens.

By now, you understand that your technological tools are not neutral; they are inducements, leading you to particular ways of being. Your digital tools and virtual environments have the power to motivate or demotivate, extend or reduce your capability, energize or de-energize you, increase or diminish your capacity, increase or decrease your dependence on those very technologies—begging the question: *Are you using the tool or is it using you?*

As we come to the close of this book, please let me speak plainly: *Beware anything that reduces your capacity*, that makes you less.

Stick with me. Stay vigilant.

The Way Forward

The pandemic of the early '20s forced us to confront the limits of comfort, convenience, and control and, for those of us open to the unearthing that took place—and privileged enough to explore what that meant for us—grew our capacity for creativity, community, and care. Carrying these good burdens of *relationship* are the key to living joyfully in our digital age.

By now you have a list of nearly 100 joys. People, places, experiences, and things that uniquely bring you alive. Let's turn to that list now.

Ask yourself: *What are the commonalities? What themes run through my joys?*

Take note.

Now, go back through your list and ask: *Does my experience of this joy require my effort or attention?*

Are you beginning to see how this works? The things that bring you the most joy involve active noticing and nurturing.

Now, one question remains: How will you adopt new habits and digital tools that support your joy for the long haul?

With wisdom and wonder, that's how.

Be Wise

I shall no longer look for better days.
—Étienne Pivert de Senancour, *Obermann*

Have you heard The Serenity Prayer?

Even if you don't know its name, you almost certainly have. In the ninety years since American theologian Reinhold Niebuhr first wrote it, it has appeared in nearly every corner of popular culture, including the form made well known by the organization Alcoholics Anonymous:

> *Grant me the serenity to accept the things*
> *I cannot change,*
> *courage to change the things I can,*
> *and wisdom to know the difference.*

Sound familiar? The Serenity Prayer is a valuable mental model for how to live well with technology because, at its heart, it's talking about cultivating wisdom.

To be wise is to be marked by deep understanding, keen discernment, and a capacity for sound judgment. The wise take time to choose a good course of action before moving ahead.

It is in those moments where we feel we don't have a choice that we in fact must decide what's most important. In that way, moments of crisis can be clarifying. Calamity has a way of restoring us to reality and kindness.[31] When the global pandemic of the early '20s quarantined cities, towns, and countries the world over, we woke from our self-sufficient slumbers and learned that

We don't need to spend much money at all.
Humanity could be better if we wanted to be.
Being kind is the only thing that matters.
We were doing too much we didn't enjoy for the sake of doing.
Our needs are far fewer than we think.
Hours in a day can increase if we just slow down.
Our families need us more than we thought they did.
Almost everything we do is non-essential.
Adversity and fear bring out the best and the worst in people. Both lurk in the deepest part of each of us, and we must decide which will prevail.
Relationships are important. Life sucks if you do it alone.

Remember?

COVID-19 was, in an all-consuming way, what Virginia Woolf has called "a moment of being," a situation that made us feel the shock of reality.[32] It made us ask ourselves some of life's most fundamental questions:

Why are we here?
What are we doing?
What does it all mean?

At many times in our lives, the unavoidable truth will be that changing our situation is necessary; the best, maybe even the only, course of action. In the wise words of poet Anaïs Nin, there comes a time in each of our lives when "the risk to remain tight in a bud was more painful than the risk it took to blossom."

The bud is a tender and quiet place. It feels safer inside than facing the crowd of challenges the outer world promises.

But the risks of blooming are worth it.

The rewards of wise, intentional change are innumerable. They may even be the greatest possible wisdom you can cultivate, the greatest gift you can give yourself and those around you.

The most joyful life is the one in which you never stop growing. But how do we get there?

My eighty-seven-year-old grandfather is living proof of the joys wisdom and wonder bring. He regularly recounts his daily three-kilometre walks, writing on Facebook: "I marvel at the beauty all around. Daffodils in their yellow cloaks and trees budding everywhere. Did see a magnolia in bloom along with robins, cardinals, geese and much more. During this pandemic we need to focus on the beauty around us and give thanks for what we *do have*."

All things bright and beautiful.

Here. Alive. Now.

As you forge ahead on open waters, you want only to be burdened by what's essential—and *real*. To adopt technology wisely, in a way that supports your tangible, real-world joys, it's essential to understand the difference between the virtual and real, what each offers and what each asks of you.

Something real reveals and is continuous with the living, beating, breathing world you can smell and touch and see. Something real cannot be experienced out of context or time: a conversation standing with your neighbour on the sidewalk, a mug held firmly in your hand. Something virtual is discontinuous; it can happen anytime or anyplace and reveals little about what matters in the world.[33] It is possible to withdraw from the virtual at any time, but you cannot withdraw from reality. Not really.

> The most joyful life is the one in which you never stop growing.

Over my decade-long journey, seeking to live joyfully with technology and leading others to do the same, I began to understand what philosopher Albert Borgmann means when he says, "Joys give life its splendor, burdens give life its grounding."

> Joys are gifts; they are easy to take. Burdens are challenges, and they can be crushing. Thus burdens require more training and thought, and there is a special complication to the task since in the prevailing culture the notion of burdens is questionable.[34]

I agree with Albert wholeheartedly. Burdens were always meant to be challenging. They have always asked much of us. But they do not have to be crushing. Not when you know the true meaning of the word *capacity*.

With wisdom, you can adopt the digital tools and habits that serve your relationships, creativity, and capacity, and confidently choose to miss out on the rest. Technology is an effort to get everything under control, but using technology as a means to unburden ourselves is just window-dressing; it distracts us from the good burden of truly living. It leaves us aimless and unmoored, left asking *What is it all for?*

Carrying the right burdens gives your life direction. Recognizing what those good burdens are and embracing them is what it is to be wise.

Carrying the right burdens gives your life direction. Recognizing what those good burdens are and embracing them is what it is to be wise.

Let us be the ones who spend our time well;
who live every hour of every day.

Quests

1. Ask yourself: do the media I consume and the digital tools I use make me wise?

2. Tip the scales in favour of the real. Spend more time offline than online today. Close the computer. Leave the phone at home. Get your hands dirty. Garden, explore, cook, care, create. Notice how you feel at the end of the day.

3. Add 20 more joys to your list.

The goal is aliveness.
The purpose is love.

Take up the good burden of being wise.

Be Amazed

The changing of the day into night, the seasons, the flowers, the fruits, and all the rest which comes to us from time to time so that we can and must enjoy them—these are the true impulses toward life on earth. The more we are open to such pleasures the happier we are. If, however, the variety of sights dances before our eyes without our taking part in them, if we are not receptive to these sacred offerings, then the great evil finds its way into us, the most severe sickness: we consider life a repulsive burden.
—Goethe

I'm sitting atop a darkened hill conversing over the crackle of a close burning fire, silently puffing my first cigar. Earlier this evening, I walked on sandalled feet following the full moon's glow to the decaying dock below. There, we shed housecoats and thrust our half-tan bodies into the shallows of the Pacific. It's midsummer, a perfectly respectable thing to do: paddling through black waters, the dart of our extremities igniting a symphony of phosphorescence.

"There are two kinds of light," wrote humorist James Thurber, "the glow that illuminates and the glare that obscures." He may well have been writing about the ocean at night. In today's light-polluted world, the beauty of the evening sky can too often be obscured by the glare of industry. But if you look closely, travel out farther, beyond the artificial light, you might see something extraordinary: the quiet glow of bioluminescence.

This naturally occurring phenomenon affects 20 percent of marine species. Ocean phosphorescence is primarily due to the plankton commonly seen at night; they emit tiny bursts of light when the water is disturbed. The flash is designed to startle or divert a predatory crustacean, allowing the plankton to escape. For centuries phosphorescence has played an important role in marine navigation, making the shoreline and shoals visible. The glow can be seen in the wake of large ships some thirty kilometres away—a halo hovering in open water.

Those who have experienced the fire of blackened waters might put it more simply: bioluminescence is like swimming with the stars.

Let Curiosity Be Your Guide

It was Christmas Eve 1993 when John Lloyd awoke to the devastating thought that the sum of all he had achieved was worthless. By all outward standards, Lloyd was the picture of success. He was a TV producer and director with homes in London and Oxfordshire, which he shared with his wife and three children. Before the age of forty, he had produced some of the most popular comedy shows in Britain and had three BAFTAs (Britain's Oscars) to show for it. But that Christmas morning, he was flattened by the sense that he didn't know anything.

"[Lloyd] entered a serious depression, despite knowing he had much to be thankful for," recounts Ian Leslie in his book, *Curious: The Desire to Know and why Your Future Depends On It*. "Lloyd eschewed some of the popular strategies for coping with male mid-life crisis." Instead, he stopped everything. He took time off work, went on long walks, read, and drank whiskey. He began doing the things he never used to have time for.

He followed his curiosity.

Lloyd learned about philosophers, ancient cultures, magnetism, and light. There was no rhyme or reason to his methods.

The further down the rabbit hole of discovery he went, the more he wanted to know. Underpinning the sheer pleasure of wondering at the world were his questions: What is the meaning of life? What is the point of me?

A few years later Lloyd pitched a new show to the BBC: *QI*, a kind of *Ripley's Believe it or Not* quiz show that became one of Britain's most popular and longest-running TV series. It's worth noting here, that the quiz show actually undermines what many others of this sort aim to do: ask a question and receive a correct answer. Instead, respondents are not necessarily rewarded for offering correct answers, but *interesting* answers. Would Lloyd have thought of this radical new idea if he hadn't taken the time to follow his own curiosity—to learn just for the sake of learning?

I have a friend, a scientist, who has a hypothesis: *the internet is fake wonder*. That's a problem because "Out of wonder," says Aristotle, "comes joy." Wherever the capacity for joy exists the capacity for wonder will be found.[35]

So, does that mean all joy experienced online is false? What about offline?

For many adults, the flame of curiosity has all but gone out. In fact, some experts say our pure intellectual zeal begins to wane as early as four years old. We hit an equilibrium and quit replenishing our stores. As a result, we have fewer questions and more default settings. "This waning curiosity is not necessarily a bad thing," says Ian Leslie. "It's essential in becoming a person who can act on the world, rather than one in thrall to it." But in his study of the inquiring mind, he has landed on an essential truth: *In the game of life, it's the curious who win.*

If you're paying attention, everything you see—from a fire beetle's underbelly to the *Magna Carta* to a pepper plant—and do—from nursing a child to growing vegetables from seed to falling in love—is extraordinary. From this vantage point, any experience can be translated into a joy—and an opportunity to contribute something beyond yourself.

The key is to be open and attentive. To know joy when you feel it.

When was the
last time you felt
wonder?

We Need One Another to Get to Good

Many of us know the thing we ought to be doing, but don't do it. We feel the pull of our curiosities, the quiet call of wonder but, like much of life: the urgent wins out. We stick to routine. Fall into ruts. Allow a troubling rigidity sap opportunities for exploration. We lose hours, weeks, months to the infinite, deadening scroll.

We know we should freshen up our painting skills. We should make that weekend drive into the country. We should join a writing group—if not for the critique, for the camaraderie. But something holds us back

Control, convenience, comfort.

Often, it's a community that gets us where we need to go.

Joining Community

One summer I uncharacteristically signed up for a "writing flash mob"—a kind of loose pop-up writing group. It was outside my comfort zone but seemed like a fun idea.

To say I narrowly made it to the first meet-up is a gross overstatement. I sheepishly shuffled up to the group—held in the farmers' market shelter in my neighbourhood—ten minutes late, in quiet awe of ten writerly neighbours fervently putting pen to paper. They took turns reading fresh lines aloud to one another—strangers. I listened, then joined in.

The lines I wrote that day were some of the loveliest and truest I'd had the courage to get down in some time. What a wonder. Curiosity and community helped get me there.

Making Space

Wonder is the opposite of stress. If community is important to our creative contributions to the world, so too is making space to marvel.

For years, tech founder and creative leader Paul Jarvis spent every spare moment in the woods, escaping his life in downtown Vancouver's bustling core. He finally had the courage to pull the plug on his urban lifestyle by moving to one of the Pacific Northwest's surfing hot spots. And he found so much more there than he'd bargained for. "One can only surf so many days," laughs Paul. "Soon you are forced to be introspective: the lens is pointed back on you."

Wonder is the opposite of stress.

This lens led him to the backwoods of an inland home where Paul spends as much time outside in his garden as he does inside creating the suite of courses, books, and products he's known for. Inside is a bit of a stretch. With floor-to-ceiling windows in his and his partner's open-concept home, it's Western red cedars and ocean as far as the eyes can see. "Now that I've had that," he says, "I feel like I need it. Space is one of the most important things—physically and mentally.

"With our minds and houses we can quickly fill it. We need to schedule time and space to explore, and just be open to what may come," says Paul. To facilitate this, he schedules full weeks of open time—no interviews, no client work, just space to play and explore, to let wonder and curiosity take the lead.

"It's just there to be open."

As important as space is to Paul, experimentation has been the linchpin of his livelihood. "I was the kid who, when he got LEGO, threw away the instructions and made whatever I wanted."

I know that kind of kid. I'm raising one.

After dropping out of second-year computer science at University of Toronto, Paul made a website for fun that exploded with popularity, then sold it. He was intrigued by electronic publishing, wondering how one might successfully write and launch an e-book. He took a crack at a vegan cookbook and continued experimenting with new formats. This led to four independently released bestsellers. Over time, Paul felt the pull to communicate what he had learned about creativity over the years.

"I wanted to share but was too scared," he remembers. "Then I decided fear was a stupid reason not to do it."

For a decade he ran *Sunday Dispatches*, a wildly popular newsletter for creatives, the Creative Class course—a masterclass before MasterClass existed—and authored numerous books, including *Company of One: Why Staying Small Is the Next Big Thing for Business*. Today, Paul is a veteran of the online tech world and runs Fathom, a privacy-focused digital analytics company working to make the internet a safer and more equitable place. His personal website, once a source of massive traffic, now simply says this: "I used to have a personal brand and online presence, and now I don't. I now work at Fathom Analytics."

He still lives in the woods.

"Long walks outdoors always make me more productive, especially when I need to get things done," says Paul. "We are not robots." For Paul, making space meant opening himself up creatively.

When you make space for the good burdens you want to nurture in your life, joy inevitably follows.

Staying Open and Storing Up

There is no exact science to curiosity, no direct return on investment. Learning is not that simple. What we know for sure is that our capacity for wonder needs nourishment.

Wonder is a posture in which we hold space for the unique impressions of our lives. There is something important we do in the storing up of things. We are sorting, sifting, making sense of our thoughts and experiences. Holding moments of wonder close, in a compulsively over-sharing digital culture, is a rare discipline. One that is necessary for creating good work.

Our capacity for wonder needs nourishment.

As poet Aaron Belz laments, "These [online] outlets, to me, feel like wraiths that suck out my secrets, my lies, my wit, and with all that my sense of what ought to be. Without those things, I can't hope to produce authentic poems."[36]

Every day we are filling our inner treasure trove of curiosities. These new ideas and experiences inspire our efforts of love. If you are stopped up, maybe you need to give a little. Maybe you need to get out of your head and into your body, away from computers and into deep waters.

Maybe you need to wade into wonder, for to wonder is to be on the way.

Let us be the ones who have joy;
who choose love over fear.

The goal is aliveness.
The purpose is love.

Take up the good burden of being amazed.

Go Forth

To seek the highest good is to live well.
—Saint Augustine

My son Thomas stopped me one day to remark about a book I had made.

"Isn't it amazing that you made this thing?" he said. "This thing that you made with your own hands? You didn't know what it would be. But didn't it become more than you thought it would be? Isn't that true, Mommy?"

Yes, Thomas. Yes, it is.

It always is.

Take up good burdens.

Drop the pebble of love and watch it ripple.

There is joy on the way, friend. Grow your capacity to be here and awake, human and you, useful and committed, grateful and brave, wise and amazed.

I believe that pursuing joy is a revolutionary act. That a life oriented toward the life-giving is, in itself, a good. Every impulse we have to wrongly shed a burden that is rightly ours to carry is to err from life.

How do you know a good burden? It makes you more.

It makes us *all* more.

My 100 Joys

1.	19.
2.	20.
3.	21.
4.	22.
5.	23.
6.	24.
7.	25.
8.	26.
9.	27.
10.	28.
11.	29.
12.	30.
13.	31.
14.	32.
15.	33.
16.	34.
17.	35.
18.	36.

My 100 Joys

37.	55.
38.	56.
39.	57.
40.	58.
41.	59.
42.	60.
43.	61.
44.	62.
45.	63.
46.	64.
47.	65.
48.	66.
49.	67.
50.	68.
51.	69.
52.	70.
53.	71.
54.	72.

My 100 Joys

73.

74.

75.

76.

77.

78.

79.

80.

81.

82.

83.

84.

85.

86.

87.

88.

89.

90.

91.

92.

93.

94.

95.

96.

97.

98.

99.

100.

Acknowledgements

This book has been many years in the making. There are many people who have made it possible. I feel deep gratitude to the following people especially:

Thank you Michael Crook. There is not one part of this book that does not have your fingerprint on it. You are wisdom and resolve. You have taught me more than anyone else about good burdens. You are my best burden. I love you.

Thank you to my children, Madeleine, Thomas, and Caleb. You show me each and every day the joys of being fully alive. It is a wonder to love and be loved by you. (I promise to be the unicorn.)

Thank you to my family, Mom and Chester, Dad and Grace, Michael, David, James, Kristen, Matthew, Lynn and Jason, Barb and Pat, and Brittany, for your enthusiasm and encouragement. That has meant the world to me.

Thank you Dr. Albert Borgmann, without whom this book would not exist. You are mentor, friend, philosopher, and guide. Knowing you and being shaped by your theology of technology has been a privilege and a joy.

Thank you to Samantha Haywood for being the greatest literary agent I could ask for. Marissa Stapley and Sarah Selecky, my magical friends, thank you for putting my work in Sam's way and for welcoming me so wholeheartedly to the Transatlantic family.

Thank you to my right hand, Rebecca Wigaard. Your steadfast belief in me and the work of JOMO is a well I return to again and again. You helped research and develop so many ideas in this book—especially the navigation metaphor and algebra of joy. Thank you.

Thank you to my editor, Whitney Moran. What can I say? It has been one of the joys of my professional life to have you as my editor on *Good Burdens*. To have worked together on this book in such unprecedented times has been a special kind of magic. The fact that I already miss working on this project with you says it all. Thank you.

Thank you to the many of you who read early iterations of the manuscript and gave feedback: I'm thinking of you, Dr. Jess Perriam, Rachel Earhard, Emily Ganzer, and Tiffany Shlain. Thank you to my patrons, especially Dr. Beth Green, Nathan and Leah Lim, Aaron Reynolds, and Andrea Pennoyer, for your steadfast support and deep belief in the importance of these conversations.

Thank you to Tamara, for sharing the dream of the ship so many years ago, and to Georgia Dow, for helping me turn the ship around.

Thank you Karen Pascal and the Henri Nouwen Society for your generous support of the My Year with Henri project.

Thank you to Sandra Javera for capturing the essence of good burdens—community, creation, and care—in the cover illustration, to Heather Bryan for such excellence in the interior design, and to Andrea Pennoyer for your typographic expertise.

Thank you to the JOMO community the world over: readers, listeners, and colleagues. You inspire me to choose this path each day: joyfully missing out on the right things to make space for good burdens—the people (you!) and projects (this book) that bring joy.

Endnotes

1 "Good genes are nice, but joy is better" by Liz Mineo, *The Harvard Gazette*, April 17, 2017. news.harvard.edu/gazette/story/2017/04/over-nearly-80-years-harvard-study-has-been-showing-how-to-live-a-healthy-and-happy-life/

2 "The Heart Grows Smarter" by David Brooks, *The New York Times*, November 5, 2012. nytimes.com/2012/11/06/opinion/brooks-the-heart-grows-smarter.html

3 Tweet by Mark Manson: "What's the biggest lesson you learned during the pandemic?" Twitter, June 14, 2020. twitter.com/IAmMarkManson/status/1272274114703745024

4 *The Road Less Travelled: A New Psychology of Love, Traditional Values, and Spiritual Growth* by Scott Peck, Touchstone: 2003.

5 *Daring Greatly: How The Courage To Be Vulnerable Transforms The Way We Live, Love, Parent, And Lead* by Brené Brown, Penguin, 2015.

6 "The average American has only one close friend — here's how we got to this point" by Emma Seppala and Peter Sims, *Business Insider*, July 16, 2017. businessinsider.com/emma-seppala-the-average-american-has-only-one-close-friend-2017-7

7 Time Spent on social networking by internet users worldwide from 2012 to 2020." *Statista*, 2021. statista.com/statistics/433871/daily-social-media-usage-worldwide

8 "An Ode to Silence: Why You Need It In Your Life," August 7, 2020. health.clevelandclinic.org/why-you-need-more-silence-in-your-life

9 "Unfriending convenience" by Christina Crook, *Christianity Today*, June 21, 2018. christianitytoday.com/ct/2018/july-august/unfriending-convenience.html?share=5zSY0JlWCRbTMEofmHvQT7y-WoY2sX6LQ

10 "The Tyranny of Convenience" by Tim Wu. *The New York Times*, February 16, 2018.

11 "Americans are wary of the role social media sites play in delivering the news" by Elisa Shearer and Elizabeth Grieco, Pew Research Center, October 2, 2019. journalism.org/2019/10/02/americans-are-wary-of-the-role-social-media-sites-play-in-delivering-the-news

12 *Daring Greatly: How The Courage To Be Vulnerable Transforms The Way We Live, Love, Parent, And Lead* by Brené Brown, Penguin, 2015.

13 Institute for Digital Civic Culture newsletter, idcconline.com.

14 "Hillary Clinton on The Return of the Prodigal Son", Oprah.com. oprah.com/omagazine/hillary-clinton-on-the-return-of-the-prodigal-son

15 *Life of the Beloved* by Henri Nouwen, Crossroad, October 2002.

16 *Reaching Out: The Three Movements of the Spiritual Life* by Henry Nouwen, Random House Canada: November 2013.

17 "The Holy inefficiency of Henri Nouwen" by Philip Yancey, *Christianity Today*, December 9, 1996. christianitytoday.com/ct/1996/december9/6te080.html

17 "The Art of self-renewal: the pioneering social scientist John Gardner on how to keep your work and spirit alive for the long run" by Maria Popova, *Brainpickings* [nd]. brainpickings.org/2014/07/14/self-renewal-gardner

18 "What Happens When We Reconnect with Nature" by Kristophe Green and Dacher Keltner, *Greater Good Magazine*, March 1, 2017.

19 "How Social Isolation Affects the Brain" by Caroline Offord, *The Scientist*, July/August 2020. the-scientist.com/features/how-social-isolation-affects-the-brain-67701

20 "Opinion: Happiness Won't Save You" by Philip Brickman,

The New York Times online, November 11, 2020. nytimes. com/2020/11/24/opinion/happiness-depression-suicide-psychology. html?action=click&module=Opinion&pgtype=Homepage

21 "Be Careful with those commitment devices" by Jodi Beggs, *Economists Do It With Models*, June 2009. economistsdoitwithmodels. com/2009/06/17/be-careful-with-those-commitment-devices

22 *Embodied Leadership: The Somatic Approach to Developing Your Leadership* by Pete Hamill, Kogan Page: June 2013.

23 *The Road Less Travelled: A New Psychology of Love, Traditional Values, and Spiritual Growth* by Scott Peck, Touchstone: 2003.

24 Jocelyn Glei, RESET Course, HurrySlowly, hurryslowly.co

25 "Dopamine, Smartphones, and You: A Battle for Your Time" by Trevor Hayes, *Harvard University: Graduate School of Arts and Sciences Blog*, May 1, 2018. sitn.hms.harvard.edu/flash/2018/dopamine-smartphones-battle-time

26 "Three in five Americans feel LONELY and workplace culture and social media is to blame, research suggests" by James Gordon, *Daily Mail*, January 23, 2020. dailymail.co.uk/news/article-7923169/Three-five-Americans-feel-LONELY-workplace-culture-social-media-blame.html

27 "Giving thanks can make you happier," Harvard Medical School, November 22, 2011. health.harvard.edu/healthbeat/giving-thanks-can-make-you-happier

28 *Glittering Vices: A New Look at the Seven Deadly Sins and their Remedies* by Rebecca Konyndyk de Young, Baker Publishing Group: 2009.

29 "Go Ahead and Fail" by Arthur C. Brooks, The Atlantic online, February 25, 2021. theatlantic.com/family/archive/2021/02/how-overcome-fear-failure/618130

30 Albert Borgmann, "On the Blessings of Calamity and the Burdens of Good Fortune," *The Hedgehog Review*, Fall 2002.

31 Virginia Woolf, "A Sketch of the Past," *Moments of Being*, ed. Jeanne Schulkind (New York: Harcourt, 1976), 70–73.

32   Albert Borgmann, "On the Blessings of Calamity and the Burdens of Good Fortune," *The Hedgehog Review*, Fall 2002.

33   Albert Borgmann, "Pointless Perfection and Blessed Burdens," October 16, 2011.

34   *Leisure: The Basis of Culture* by Josef Pieper, Liberty Fund, Pantheon Books, Inc. 1952 (p.107).

35   "Untrending" by Aaron Belz, *Curator Magazine*, August 3, 2015. curatormagazine.com/aaronbelz/untrending

Join the Conversation

For Book Clubs

Find the *Good Burdens* Book Club Discussion Guide and other free resources at: christinacrook.com/goodburdens.

Join Navigate

We are all going to navigate technology for the rest of our lives but we get to decide *how*. Try Navigate, my digital well being program to beat FOMO and keep focus. Get one month free with code *goodburdens* at christinacrook.com/navigate.

The JOMO Manifesto

The "Let us be the ones…" lines at the end of each chapter comprise the ten commitments of The JOMO Manifesto. Learn more and get your own letterpress print at experiencejomo.com.